Gautama Buddha

Zane M. Diamond

Gautama Buddha

Education for Wisdom

Springer

Zane M. Diamond
Faculty of Education
Monash University
Frankston, VIC, Australia

ISBN 978-981-16-1764-5 ISBN 978-981-16-1765-2 (eBook)
https://doi.org/10.1007/978-981-16-1765-2

This Springer imprint is published by the registered company Springer Nature Singapore Pte Ltd.
The registered company address is: 152 Beach Road, #21-01/04 Gateway East, Singapore 189721, Singapore

Funding Support Acknowledgement

Research such as this does not occur without financial and research infrastructure support.

I want to acknowledge the financial support for this project over nearly 30 years starting with an Australian Ph.D. scholarship and an Australian Government Research in Asia Award 1994–1996 that supported me to undertake my Ph.D. in Thailand with the expectation that I contribute to Australia's efforts to better engage with its Asian neighbours.

To the generosity of the donors of the Phayon-Thonghau Eiamlapa Award for supporting my research regarding the transferability of Theravādan Buddhist pedagogies in teacher education between Thailand and Australia and for their ongoing support with the underpinning research for this monograph, I offer my deepest gratitude.

I also want to acknowledge the Faculty of Education, Monash University for their ongoing support for this project with gratitude and profound thanks. As a research-intensive faculty, I have been given access to research infrastructure, time, and research funding to pursue my understanding of how the pathway to the development of inner wisdom can be transplanted from these ancient roots into modern, multicultural, Australia with its vibrant diversity and larrikin spirit. I am grateful each day for this continued support and encouragement.

May the benefit of this work be shared with all sentient beings for the good of all.

Paṭhamapuññābhisandasutta

Mahodadhiṃ aparimitaṃ mahāsaraṃ,
Bahubheravaṃ ratanavarānamālayaṃ;
Najjo yathā naragaṇasaṅghasevitā,
Puthū savantī upayanti sāgaraṃ.
Evaṃ naraṃ annadapānavatthadaṃ,
Seyyānisajjattharaṇassa dāyakaṃ;
Puññassa dhārā upayanti paṇḍitaṃ,
Najjo yathā vārivahāva sāgaran"ti.
(AN 4.51, SuttaCentral 2020, paras 11 & 12)

Streams of Merit

Just as the many rivers used by the hosts of people,
flowing downstream, reach the ocean,
the great mass of water, the boundless sea,
the fearsome receptacle of heaps of gems;
so the streams of merit reach the wise man
who is a giver of food, drink, and cloth;
they reach the donor of beds, seats, and covers
like rivers carrying their waters to the sea.
(AN 4.51, SuttaCentral 2020, paras 11 & 12, Bhikkhu Bodhi, Trans.)

References

SuttaCentral. (2020). Aṅguttara Nikāya 4.51. *Paṭhamapuññābhisandasutta.* Retrieved December 31 2020 from https://suttacentral.net/an4.51/pli/ms. Pāli text from the Mahāsaṅgīti Tipiṭaka Buddhavasse 2500: World Tipiṭaka Edition in Roman Script. Edited and published by The M.L. Maniratana Bunnag Dhamma Society Fund, 2005. Based on the digital edition of the Chaṭṭha

Saṅgāyana published by the Vipassana Research Institute, with corrections and proofreading by the Dhamma Society.
SuttaCentral. (2020). Aṅguttara Nikāya 4.51. Streams of Merit. Retrieved December 31 2020 from https://suttacentral.net/an4.51/en/bodhi. © Bhikkhu Bodhi, The Numerical Discourses of the Buddha (Wisdom Publications, 2012). This excerpt from The Numerical Discourses of the Buddha by Bhikkhu Bodhi is licensed under a Creative Commons Attribution-NonCommercial-NoDerivs 3.0 Unported License. Based on the work The Numerical Discourses of the Buddha at Wisdom Publications. Permissions beyond the scope of this license may be available at Wisdom Publications. Prepared for H by Blake Walsh.

Acknowledgments

I dedicate this work to all past teachers of the Buddha's pathway to the development of inner wisdom, in particular, my teacher Ayya Khema Bhikkhuni (August 25, 1923–November 2, 1997), and the monks and nuns of the many temples and monasteries who have guided my understanding of the Buddha and his teachings. They taught me how to understand the Buddha's teachings and explained to me and showed me their methods of teaching the *Buddha-Dhamma*. I offer them a deep respect for their painstaking work to carry the *Buddha-Dhamma* into the 21st century in a way that we can still be guided by it towards *nibbāna* enlightenment. I offer my sincere thanks for their willingness to allow me to live and study amongst them in forest monasteries and retreat centres in Thailand, Germany, and Australia.

I offer my gratitude to the laypeople who support these precious centres of teaching, learning, preservation, and transmission. To the teachers and academics in modern education systems, in early years centres, schools, and universities trying to maintain a pathway in their work towards developing inner wisdom in their students, I offer my appreciation and respect.

I want to thank all my Thai friends and colleagues in Thailand and Australia who, since the early years of my studies in Thailand, have guided my understanding of Thai Buddhism and how it is taught in the mainstream formal Thai school and university systems. To Professors Soraj Hongladarom and Krisadawan Hongladarom, to my Phitsanulok family, the Suttisans, particularly my Thai sister Nong Jaaw who tragically passed away too young. To the monks and nuns of Wat Suan Mokkh (https://www.suanmokkh-idh.org/) for teaching me the true nature of *Buddha-Dhamma*, I extend my most profound respect and gratitude.

I would like to thank the Japan International Education Society for their generous encouragement for me to present my research over these past years and their warmth and engagement in guiding me in the Japanese Way, 深い感謝と感謝の気持ちを込めて with deep appreciation and gratitude. In particular, sincere thanks to Professor Keijiro Tanaka, his son, Professor Junichi Tanaka, and Professor Chizu Sato, for sharing their wisdom and their gift of guidance with my grappling with the interplay of traditional, Indigenous, and Buddhist educational philosophy in Japan.

I also want to thank the monks, nuns, lay teachers and educators for their willingness to participate in this research. I have bothered many people over these past

40 years, too many to mention, each of whom have shared their piece of this jigsaw about the pathway to developing wisdom in the modern world. May you all share in the merit of this work. In particular, I want to acknowledge Professor Bob Teasdale, who saw the merit of my curiosity about the pedagogies for developing wisdom all those years ago as my Ph.D. mentor. Gratitude also to Ānandajoti Bhikkhu for his thorough and reliable research and the excellent maps he has generously shared with me for this monograph (Bhante Ānandajoti: https://www.ancient-buddhist-texts.net/Miscellaneous/About.htm).

To the myriad translators of the *Buddha-Dhamma* over these past 2,500 years, I owe the deepest gratitude. Having access to printed copies of the Buddha's teachings in a language that I can understand i s aremarkable thing. In particular, I want to thank the translators and donors of the Pāli Text Society, on whose English translations of the *Tipitaka* Buddhist Canon I have come to rely (http://www.pāḷitext.com/). To the Buddhist Publication Society (https://www.bps.lk/index.php) for their sustained dissemination of English language versions of literature in hard copy, books and leaflets that I still treasure, that came into my hands in my teenage years, thank you. That I can share these hard copies in professional development workshops with Australian teachers and university academics is something of a miracle.

I am also deeply indebted to the magnificent digitization work being undertaken at SuttaCentral. I acknowledge those who have contributed to the significant work of Mahāsaṅgīti Tipiṭaka Buddhavasse 2500: World Tipiṭaka Edition in Roman Script. Edited and published by The M.L. Maniratana Bunnag Dhamma Society Fund, 2005. Based on the digital edition of the Chaṭṭha Saṅgāyana published by the Vipassana Research Institute, with corrections and proofreading by the Dhamma Society. To the translators of the Pāli, in particular Bhikkhu Sujato, Bhikkhu Bodhi, Bhikkhu Brahmali, and Bhikkhu Ānandajoti whose translations into English I have relied on for many of the quotations across these chapters, and for their determined, sustained commitment to the preservation and dissemination of the *Tipitaka*, its commentaries and translations into the numerous languages that now carry the teachings of the Buddha to the world—thank you. To the Buddhist Publication Society (https://www.bps.lk/index.php) for their donors' generosity, thank you for now providing digital access to many of your publications—with thanks for being preservers of the *Buddha-Dhamma* and reliable guides.

I also want to acknowledge and thank the Daylesford Dharma School, Victoria, Australia. Now entering its twelfth year, it is a school that is developing its pathway to teaching in a manner inspired by the teachings of the Buddha and using the pedagogical approaches that he developed. I want to acknowledge Andrea Furness, Chair of the School Board and one of the school's founders, the School Board members, teachers and staff past and present, and the Dharma Education Sub-Committee members, chaired by Dr. Sue Smith. Slowly, together, we are working out how to support the Buddha's teachings to thrive in Australia's fertile soil while maintaining the enduring spirit of the Buddha's educational philosophy at the core.

I also acknowledge audiences, reviewers and editors of publications over the past years who have sharpened my thinking and scholarship. The published works I have quoted and referred to in this edition, have brought the Buddha's ideas into new focus:

Chapter 1

Ma Rhea, Z. (2018). Teaching and Learning for Multicultural Societies: Reimagining Pedagogical Content Knowledge, *Journal of International Education*, Japan, Vol. 24, pp. 87–98. Retrieved on December 31 2020 at https://www.jstage.jst.go.jp/article/jies/24/0/24_87/_article/-char/en.

Chapter 2

Anderson, P. J., Maeda, K., Diamond, Z. M. and Sato, C. (Eds). (2021). *Post-Imperial Perspectives on Indigenous Education: Lessons from Japan and Australia*. Routledge.
Ma Rhea, Z. (2017). *Wisdom, Knowledge, and the Postmodern University in Thailand. Palgrave Macmillan.* (Online publication details: http://www.palgrave.com/gp/book/9781137382924.)
Ma Rhea, Z. (2017). Buddhist Pedagogy in Teacher Education: Cultivating Wisdom by Skilful Means, *Asia-Pacific Journal of Teacher Education*, 1–18, Retrieved on December 31 2020 at https://doi.org/10.1080/1359866X.2017.1399984.
Ma Rhea, Z. (2013). Buddhist Wisdom and Modernisation: Finding the balance in globalized Thailand. *Globalizations*, 10(4), 635–650. Retrieved on December 31 2020 at https://doi.org/10.1080/14747731.2013.806739.
Ma Rhea, Z. (2010). Transmorphosis: Negotiating Discontinuities in Academic Work, *Policy Futures in Education*, 8(6), 632–643.

Chapter 3

Diamond, Z. (2020). Hiyoku na dojō o motomete: furukute atarashii bukkyō no kyōjyuhō, karikyuramu, kyōzai (Tanaka, J. Trans.), *Journal of International Education Society*, No. 26, pp. 144–145.
Ma Rhea, Z. (2012). Thinking Galtha, Teaching Literacy: From Aboriginal Mother Tongue to Strangers' Texts and Beyond in Cree, A. (Ed). *Aboriginal Education: New Pathways for Teaching and Learning*. Berowra: Australian Combined University Press, 24–53.
Ma Rhea, Z. (2002). 'The Economy of Ideas: Colonial Gift and Postcolonial Product' in A. Quayson and DT Goldberg (Eds). *Relocating Postcoloniality* London, UK: Blackwells, 205–16.
Ma Rhea, Z. (1999). 'Separate domains or hybrid worldview? Women's Liberation and Vimokkha Spiritual Liberation', *Australian Journal of Feminist Studies* 14(30), 281–91.
Ma Rhea, Z. (1997). Gift, Commodity and Mutual Benefit: Analysing the Transfer of University Knowledge between Thailand and Australia'. *Higher Education*

Policy: The Quarterly Journal of the International Association of Universities, 10(2), pp. 111–20.
Ma Rhea, Z. (1997). University Knowledge Exchange: Gift, Commodity and Mutual Benefit' *Californian Sociologist* 17/18, pp. 211–50.
Ma Rhea, Z. (1995). Changing Manifestations of Wisdom and Knowledge in Thailand'. *Prospects* 25(4), December, pp. 669–82.
Ma Rhea, Z. (1994). Secular Postmodernity and Buddhist Modernisation: Australia and Thailand'. In *Religion Literature and the Arts*. Edited by Michael Griffith, Sydney, Australia: Berget Pty. Ltd., pp. 340–6.

Chapter 4

Ma Rhea, Z. (2012). Mindful Teaching: Laying the Dharma Foundations for Buddhist Education in Australia, *International Education Journal: Comparative Perspectives*, 11(1), pp. 35–51.
Ma Rhea, Z. (2001). Approaches to the development of critical analysis in the university: The impact of culture. *Manyusa: Journal of the Humanities and Social Sciences*, 1–2: 97-126.

Chapter 5

Anderson, P. J., Diamond, Z. & Diamond, J. (2018). Preservation and maintenance of Indigenous histories, languages, and cultures: The role of education, *Journal of the Japanese Association for the Study of Learning Society*, Japan, Vol. 14, pp. 26–35. Retrieved on December 31 2020 at https://www.jstage.jst.go.jp/article/gakusyusyakai/14/0/14_26/_article/-char/en.
Ma Rhea, Z. (2014). Higher Education for a Wise Life: Wisdom Traditions and the Modern University in Alvares, C. (Ed.). *Multicultural Knowledge and the University*, India: Multiversity and Penang: Citizens International, Chapter 6, 159–173.
Ma Rhea, Z. (2004). The preservation and maintenance of the knowledge of Indigenous peoples and local communities: The role of education in *Journal of Australian Indigenous Issues*. 7(1), 3–18.
Teasdale, G.R. and Ma Rhea, Z. (Eds). (2000). *Local Knowledge and Wisdom in Higher Education*. UK, USA: Pergamon Elsevier.

To my wife, Jeane Diamond, whose deep wisdom and keen mind have enlivened this writing project, to you I will always owe debt of deep gratitude and thanks. To Prasadi Hatanwila Liyana Arachchige, my research assistant whose penetrating questions and clarifications have greatly contributed to my ideas being able to be expressed clearly; thank you for your commitment to the preservation of an accurate transmission of *Buddha-Dhamma*. To Andrea Furness, for reading versions of this manuscript with your keen *Dharma* mind and heart—as always thank you for your generous trust and support.

And finally, I want to thank Professor Paul Gibbs, Series Editor of the *Key Thinkers in Education*, an academic series published by Springer and all the publication team at Springer for their support, encouragement and flexibility to allow me the time and intellectual space to focus on this fascinating topic. To Professor Gibbs, I am indebted to you for this opportunity.

Frankston South
2020

Professor Zane M. Diamond

Contents

About the Author

Professor Zane M. Diamond I have been researching the relationship between Buddhism and education since 1992 and was a student of Ven. Ayya Khema Bhikkhuni (now deceased). I am a recognised Dhamma teacher in the Theravada tradition, am also a qualified teacher, and an academic in the Faculty of Education at Monash University.

I have nearly 30 years of teaching experience spanning primary, university, government, and corporate education. My teaching has been shaped by the context of my experiences in a remote Anangu (Aboriginal) desert school, as a lecturer at various universities, as a strategic organizational change educator with Australian corporations, and as a program leader for international leadership and management development courses.

My research investigates how inner wisdom might be developed in modern education and professional development, addressing the alienation from mainstream education that people from non-dominant cultures report. I observe that full participation as citizens requires that education enables the inclusion of diverse student needs and histories by understanding the impact of ancestry, ethnicity, and lifeways on providing mainstream education services. Full participation as citizens also requires that children and young adults are encouraged to develop their inner wisdom, laying firm foundations for ongoing personal development through adulthood. Citizens with inner wisdom can engage optimistically and capably with the future.

I research the sociology of education (sub-fields of leadership and pedagogical reform) and am inclusive and comparativist in approach. I employ theoretical perspectives drawn from Indigenist, Buddhist, social exchange, organizational change, and intelligent complex adaptive systems theories to understand how to incorporate a diversity of ethnoreligious cultural perspectives about wisdom within mainstream education and in the leadership and management of education services.

My research is guiding the emergence of new forms of wisdom education to address contemporary issues, involving students and young adults, parents, teachers, education bureaucrats, and teacher educators both in Australia and across the Indo-Asia-Oceania region. I am finding that the impact of diverse ethnoreligious cultural expectations on education is as pressing in India, Malaysia, Japan, Australia, Sri Lanka, Thailand, China, and Samoa. The missing element across all ethnoreligious cultures is the disappearance of the cultivation of stillness from which inner wisdom can arise.

My research scope encompasses: embedding Indigenous and traditional wisdom pedagogies into the work of modern universities, schools, and other public service organizations, particularly emphasising how cultures develop stillness in their traditional education systems; developing pluriculturally-appropriate pedagogies for stillness education; negotiating Indigenous traditional environmental knowledge into new approaches to sustainable and wise land, water, and food education; and, an overarching study of the pedagogies of inner wisdom development for communities, universities, and schools.

List of Figures

List of Tables

Chapter 1
Introduction—Gautama Buddha in Historical Context

Abstract The introductory chapter sets the scene for exploring the life of the Buddha as a teacher, the development of his teachings, and his teaching approach; the contemporary context of education, where immigrants from may ethnoreligious traditions have established the many traditions of Buddhism across the globe, an introduction to the Buddha as a person, a spiritual archetype, and, the focus of this monograph, as an educational theorist and notable teacher of how humans can develop inner wisdom.

Keywords Buddha · Teaching · Education theory · Wisdom

1.1 Introducing the Buddha as a Teacher

It is somewhat unusual to examine the Buddha's legacy as an educational theorist and exemplary teacher. Much has been written about the life and the spiritual teachings of the Buddha over the last 2,500 years, but very few think about his work as a teacher. Countless commentaries have been written about his life as a historical and spiritual figure, in many languages, preserved in many traditions. This book's focus takes these aspects into account and focuses on the Buddha as a significant educational thinker and a teacher of enduring renown. Even during the Buddha's time, it was recognised that he brought a distinctive skill to his journey of spiritual development: he was blessed with the skills, knowledge, and understanding of his experiences such that he could teach others. In the Buddhist Canon, there are references to individuals who became a *pacceka-buddha* defined as being 'one enlightened by himself, i.e. one who has attained the supreme and perfect insight but dies without proclaiming the truth to the world' (SuttaCentral, 2020b, para. 3). By distinction, Gautama Siddhārtha, the historical Buddha considered in this text, was recognised as a *samma sambuddha.* He was able to teach what he had learned. In the *Sammāsambuddhasutta* (SN 22.58, SuttaCentral, 2020, paras. 3–8), the Buddha explains the distinction as being:

> *"Therein, bhikkhus, what is the distinction, what is the disparity, what is the difference between the Tathagata, the Arahant, the Perfectly Enlightened One, and a bhikkhu liberated by wisdom?"* ...
>
> ... *The Blessed One said this:*

Z. M. Diamond, *Gautama Buddha*, https://doi.org/10.1007/978-981-16-1765-2_1

> *"The Tathagata, bhikkhus, the Arahant, the Perfectly Enlightened One, is the originator of the path unarisen before, the producer of the path unproduced before, the declarer of the path undeclared before. He is the knower of the path, the discoverer of the path, the one skilled in the path. And his disciples now dwell following that path and become possessed of it afterwards."*
>
> *"This, bhikkhus, is the distinction, the disparity, the difference between the Tathagata, the Arahant, the Perfectly Enlightened One, and a bhikkhu liberated by wisdom."*

It is also unusual to employ the modern language of education about teaching and learning, curriculum, pedagogy, and formative assessment to consider the Buddha's contributions to the human weal. The knowledge he held and taught, as discussed in this book, is ancient. The Buddha accepted a vocation to teach that became his life until he died, a career spanning 45 years. His long teaching career stands in marked distinction with others whose teaching span was considerably shorter, such as Jesus Christ, and more recent, such as the teachings of the Prophet Mohammed, even as their spiritual teachings have also gone on to be developed into formalised religions. The more ancient Judaic, Upanishadic, Brahmanical, and Jain traditions shared many similarities, with their teaching and learning approaches recorded in their respective sacred texts but, as will be discussed throughout this book, distinct from the Buddha's approach. There are several unique aspects to the Buddha as an education thinker and teacher that distinguish his teaching methods and curriculum for the development of inner wisdom from earlier traditions and those that have followed.

Over his 45 years of teaching, like any good teacher, he developed an impressive corpus of knowledge about his experiences of his path to inner spiritual development and *nibbāna* enlightenment that he was able to refine into a practical and scalable pedagogical approach. To some extent, he undertook refinements through daily practice and reflection. He also engaged daily with disciples and other learners in well-documented teacher-learner interface where it is possible to see the emergence and development of his teaching style. It is worth considering his educational ideas simply because a career of 45 years as a teacher is impressive, and few people manage to teach for these many years. In addition to this, his teachings and his pedagogy have managed to survive into the contemporary era with surprising relevance and, I would argue, of ongoing usefulness to the modern school teacher and university lecturer. That his work has spread from its traditional region in Northern India where he taught first, also regarded as the 'heartland' of his teachings, then spreading by word-of-mouth across Asia north, east, and south and to Greece in the East, and more recently to the West under conditions of globalisation and migration, should command respect and interest of any educationalist. The Buddha offered education innovation in philosophical and psychological terms, conveyed through an approach of profound impact. People, young and old, continue to find the Buddha's teachings useful, and this monograph introduces the Buddha as an influential educationalist with big ideas and sound pedagogical methods.

Globally, formal educations systems of schooling and higher education are failing. Previously, I have argued that together with other educators, we need to focus more on the development of wisdom in our students (Ma Rhea, 2017a, 2017b). I have investigated the potential of pedagogy inspired by the Buddha's educational philosophy to inform teacher education and the teaching profession in a global economy where nations are experiencing rapidly-changing demographics alongside cultural, social, economic, and political upheaval. I have argued that education's purpose is under scrutiny as monolithic, nation state-defined approaches to education that were developed out of colonial or anti-colonial logic and nation-building are vying with insistent, emergent questions asked by globalised, postmodern, postcolonial, postimperial students: Why are you teaching us this? What use is it? What use is what we are learning when our lives are being torn apart by global pandemics, ethnoreligious wars, and the threat of planetary destruction?

My response to these questions is an age-old one that students need to develop their inner wisdom alongside their more mundane, cognitive studies. The pathway to the cultivation of inner wisdom needs to be brought into the contemporary education malaise We need to refocus our attention beyond narrow political and econometric determinants of our curriculum and pedagogies to the development of inner wisdom in ourselves as educators, and by doing so, assist our students to lay the foundations for the development of their inner wisdom through cognitively and affectively appropriate methods. It is here that the education ideas of the Buddha excel attested to through the experiential practices of millions of humans over the last 2,500 years.

Informing this book and my quest to bring inner wisdom development explicitly into my teaching, whether face to face or virtually, are the answers given to me by my students in initial teacher education programmes, participants in corporate leadership development workshops and teacher professional development retreats, and senior government policymakers and university leaders to the questions I ask them: What will encourage you to learn about the development of your inner wisdom? What can I offer you? What do you need to know or do to have confidence that this is a reliable path? As we explore these questions, I find that almost everyone is motivated by learning about well-being, meditation, and resilience. As I canvass the ideas about the development of inner wisdom presented in this book, they become engaged and disciplined learners who are excited about developing their inner wisdom and about the education ideas of the Buddha that they can use to guide their students and their organisations. I speak to them about the pedagogy behind this approach, and week after week, we check in with their ideas and discoveries. We talk about what happened on their practicum, in their classroom or workplace, and discern together what evidence they saw of the development of their inner wisdom and how they are then modelling different behaviour and approach to their life and work. They come to such encounters engaged and excited by their discoveries, seeing evidence of their personal growth.

I am also working with teachers whose performance and the achievements of their students are judged by outcomes-based, metric-driven measures, and yet they work in organisations that are aspiring to the holistic development of students. They are including meditation, well-being, and mindfulness programmes as part of this holistic approach but there is little structuring of the content of such activities beyond the personal experiences and expertise in teaching such approaches held by the individual teacher. Teachers know there is a need, but guidance drawn from a reliable source is harder to establish. In the Buddha's teachings, I have found such a reliable pathway to support my work because he was specific in his assurance that his pedagogy and content have the development of inner wisdom at its heart.

Located in Australia, a trained social worker, teacher, and now working as an initial teacher educator at Monash University, over these last 40 years I have witnessed significant changes in the ethnic and religious composition of Australian society. In response to these changes, I have seen shifts and changes in how Australia has approached the idea of multicultural education. I am in teacher education, and we know that the challenge for teacher educators lies in their responses to the set of challenges facing them as they prepare the next generation of school teachers within complex, multicultural states. Many of the challenges were identified in the *Brundtland Report* (The World Commission on Environment and Development, 1987). This report provided something of a watershed moment in thinking about the future of education in multicultural, multiracial, multiethnic, multireligious nations (see also Beare & Slaughter, 1993; Ma Rhea & Teasdale, 2000).

Australia, together with other lands that were colonised over the last 450 years, now experiences an influx of immigrant philosophies and ways of life that are neither Indigenous nor administratively asserted during the formations of colonial nations. In the case of Australia, the ideas of the Buddha meet settler colonialism rather that Indigenous lifeways as it was in the first and second waves of expansion (see later chapters for a more detailed discussion of these waves).

The Australian education system, as is also the case with other English and French colonies and ex-colonies, was designed and developed by the white settler and other white immigrant communities from predominantly Christian religions. Approaches to education, the establishment and development of mainstream, formal education systems in many parts of the world have been shaped by this past.

Where do Buddha-inspired perspectives about education, and the cultivation of inner wisdom as education's highest purpose, fit into this picture?

1.2 The Historical Context of the Person

Conze (1957, pp. 34–38) provides a helpful approach to introduce the reader to the Buddha. He rightly points out that the Buddha's life that would be familiar to any person brought up in Asia or with Asian cultural values but that such familiarity is not reflected in Western understanding, that it is 'anything but obvious … [to most Westerners] … and requires careful explanation' (Conze, 1957, p. 34). He suggests considering the Buddha's life from three points of view: as a human being, as a spiritual principle, and as something in between the two. I have found it useful to follow this advice for Western readers and make explicit what aspects of traditional Asian and Indigenous cultural values I feel are worthy of note in the examination of the Buddha as an educationalist.

First, I make brief comment about the use of different languages in this book. While this monograph is predominantly written in Australian English, it draws on words and ideas that have been expressed by the Buddha in Sanskrit, Pal, and probably several other dialects and languages spoken in the region where he taught (for more detailed discussion, see *Glossary*, Appendix A and *Defining and shaping the Buddha's education theories from Pāḷi and Sanskrit into English* Appendix B and Chap. 2, this edition).

1.2.1 As Human Being

Based on all the information available, it does not seem to be possible to date the Buddha's life exactly and reliably (Carrithers, 1983; Conze, 1957; Laumakis, 2008; Narada Maha Thera, 2012). There are strong indications that he lived in the fifth century BCE in the north-eastern region of what is now known as India. For this discussion, I will give dates for each significant event in Siddhārtha's human life to enable the reader to understand the timespan of his teaching career. I accept that the actual dates vary from the generally accepted beginning of his life in the sixth to fourth centuries BCE, but there is less disagreement about when the sequence of life milestones happened, and for this monograph, this is the more important aspect to highlight. As a teacher, I have a philosophy that the content of what I teach must be mobilised with what I call 'provisional certainty'. To teach something, it must contain enough 'facts' or solid pieces of instruction to support learning. The art of teaching focuses students' attention on those aspects that most support learning, rather than bamboozling them with arbitrary possibilities that remain the preserve of expert scholars. For this book, I beg forgiveness of these experts as I try to speak with clarity about the essential aspects of the Buddha's life, his teaching approach and core curriculum for spiritual development.

As such, I start this discussion with the date of c.491 BCE when the Buddha was born and given the name Siddhārtha Gautama. He was born in Lumbini Park in Kapilavatthu in modern-day Nepal on the border with India. The name Gautama, or Gotama as it is sometimes spelt in English, is his family name and he was born into the *Śākya* clan into a family that were tribal clan leaders or as some might describe it, the aristocratic class. I think the claims to aristocracy and royalty may be overstated, according to contemporary understandings of these terms, but the *Tipitaka* Buddhist Canon, in translation and in a variety of languages, often accords him honorific titles such as Prince Siddhartha.

Laumakis (2008, p. 6) summarises the accepted scholarly view that '... [he] had a privileged youth, a sound moral upbringing, and a good education'. For some, Buddha, the person was born into political upheaval and war. He was possibly taught the art of war and educated in the Brahmanical tradition. As a member of a tribal clan, it is also possible that his life was not drawn into these aspects of the lives of those governed by kings. However, it would appear that the *Śākya* clan was involved in the significant social changes that were occurring as independent tribal clans, living in what Davids (1911, p. 2) termed 'free republics', were being assimilated into the emerging monarchies. As such, it is likely that the young Siddhārtha Gautama would have been influenced by war, Brahmanism, and the political changes impacting the lives of his clan.

He would have spoken Sanskrit and probably several Prakrits including Pāḷi. According to Sujato and Brahmali (2015), there is substantial evidence to suggest that there was significant socio-economic change occurring in the region where Siddhārtha lived, with small clans being brought into feudal arrangements with emergent feudal kings trying to control the development of emerging commercial town centres and regional economies in their favour. For those of this view, it makes sense that a well-educated young prince, weary of battles and scholarship and dissatisfied with the explanations that had been given to him might turn away from such upheaval and decide to look within for more profound answers to the meaning of life.

For others, Siddhārtha had lived many previous lives perfecting himself through aeons and countless reincarnations. During his long journey through countless lives that, according to Conze (1957, p. 35) 'staggers imagination', Siddhārtha had shared the fate of all living beings and so understood the depth of suffering in its infinite manifestations. In this understanding of the human incarnation of Siddhārtha, he was born auspiciously into a very protected family situation, and it was only in him witnessing a sick man, an old man, and a corpse as a young adult that he realised that even with all of the privileges of his life, he would inevitably also experience sickness, old age, and death. This realisation provoked him on the path of seeking a deeper meaning to this existence than material, mundane world pleasures that he now knew to be deeply dissatisfying.

Whether he left home as a disaffected republican tribal man of independence, a battle-weary clan warrior, or as a dissatisfied seeker, or possibly a combination of all these, in c.462 BCE at the age of 29, he left the protection of his clan and family estates and became a wandering ascetic. He undertook many extreme practices that promised to develop him spiritually. He quickly mastered many of the teachings and continued to be dissatisfied with the experiences and explanations he was being given. Ultimately, he undertook to sit in meditative and discernment practices, go inward, trust his experiences, and either breakthrough to a more satisfying spiritual level or die in his attempt. After eight long years of extreme practices, physically, psychologically, and emotionally, he broke through to what he called the *Majjhima Patipada* Middle Way. From c.456 BCE in the year of his *nibbāna* enlightenment until c.411 BCE when he died, he taught this path to the liberation of suffering for 45 years as an approach to education to develop inner wisdom.

1.2.2 As a Spiritual Principle

The Buddha is accepted as being a historical figure, but the ongoing interest in his philosophy derives in large part from the authority he commanded as a *kalyāṇamitta* reliable spiritual guide. I am using the term *kalyāṇamitta* as it is understood to mean 'a person of fine qualities who is a friend, esp. in helping one to progress spiritually by his/her example and advice' (SuttaCentral, 2020a). In the *Upaḍḍhasutta* (SN 45.2,

SuttaCentral, 2020, paras. 1–3), the Buddha himself said that such noble friendship 'is the entire holy life' explaining it this way to Ānanda:

> *Thus, have I heard. On one occasion the Blessed One was dwelling among the Śākyans where there was a town of the Śākyans named Nagaraka. Then the Venerable Ānanda approached the Blessed One. Having approached, he paid homage to the Blessed One, sat down to one side, and said to him:*
>
> *"Venerable sir, this is half of the holy life, that is, good friendship, good companionship, good comradeship."*
>
> *"Not so, Ānanda! Not so, Ānanda! This is the entire holy life".*

Demonstrating a manifestation of an evolved spiritual principle was a vital aspect at the time of the Buddha. Many teachers were proclaiming diverse approaches to human spiritual development in both the established Upanishadic and Brahmanical traditions and similarly emerging possibilities such as Jainism. The Buddha grounded his legitimacy as embodying spiritual reliability through personal experience and also, as Conze (1957, p. 36) notes, the Buddha was recognised as 'just one in an endless series of innumerable *Tathagatas* who appear throughout the ages in the world and always proclaim the same doctrine'. Importantly for the world, as the *Dhammacakkappavattanasutta* affirms, he was also recognised as having an even more remarkable capacity to be a wheel-turning Buddha (SN 56.11, SuttaCentral, 2020) a *samma sambuddha* enlightened teacher who enabled a new era of understanding to occur as the material conditions of the world were changing.

1.2.3 As Something Between the Two: Becoming a **Kalyāṇamitta** *Teacher*

The importance placed on the spiritual principle manifested by the Buddhas life work leads me to digress from Conze's third aspect of considering the Buddha in his glorified body to highlight an aspect that I believe is barely recognised but important for this book. Over many years, I have examined and undertaken an analysis of the Early Buddhist Texts (EBTs), as discussed in the previous section, and propose that what lays between the Buddha as a person and as a spiritually evolved archetype is his deep humanity and skill as a teacher. In his teaching approach and content, he demonstrates his humanness and his spiritually evolved being each day, as described extensively in the EBTs.

Having undertaken many spiritual trainings while growing up, committing his life as a wandering ascetic at age 29, the Buddha achieved *nibbāna* enlightenment in his 37th year. Initially, he was not inclined to teach. For six weeks after his *nibbāna* enlightenment, he simply absorbed the understandings that he had experienced and began to make sense of them. He was cautious about trying to teach something that had taken him so many long years to understand, hesitant to speak of his experiences and *nibbāna* enlightenment, and certainly not planning to develop a world religion.

I quote Narada Maha Thera (1992, pp. 13–14) here in detail to provide direct insight into how the Buddha decided to become a teacher of the Dharma.

> *The close of the fasting period, as the Buddha was engaged in solitary meditation, He thought: -*
>
> *"With difficulty have I apprehended the Dhamma. There is no need to proclaim it now. This Dhamma is not easily understood by those who are overcome by lust and hatred. The lust-ridden, shrouded by the mass darkness, do not see this Dhamma, which goes against the stream, abstruse, profound, difficult to perceive, and subtle."*
>
> *Eventually, His mind turned into inaction, and not to the teaching of the Dhamma.*
>
> *Thereupon a celestial being named Brahma Sahampati read the thoughts of the Blessed One, and fearing that the world might perish through not hearing the Dhamma, approached the Buddha and invited Him to teach the Dhamma.*
>
> *He wisely remarked:*
>
> *"In ancient times there arose in Magadha a Dhamma, impure, evolved by the corrupted. Open this Door to the Deathless. May they hear the Dhamma, understood by the Stainless! Just as one standing on the summit of a rocky mountain would behold the people around, even so, may the All-Seeing Wise One ascend this palace of Dhamma!"*
>
> *"May the Sorrow less One look upon the people plunged in grief and overcome by birth and decay."*
>
> *"Rise, O Hero, the victor in battle, the caravan-leader, the debt-free One, and wander in the world! May the Blessed One propound the Dhamma! There will be those who will understand the Doctrine!"*
>
> *When Brahma Sahampati entreated the Buddha for the third time, He surveyed the world with His Buddha Vision.*
>
> *On surveying the world, He perceived beings with little as well as much dust in their eyes, with keen and dull intellect, with good and bad characteristics, who are easy and difficult to be taught, and a few others who live perceiving the dangers of evil and of a future life.*
>
> *The Buddha, therefore, accepted the invitation of Brahma Sahampati and said:*
>
> *"Opened to them are the Doors to the Deathless. Let those who have ears repose confidence. Being aware of the weariness of it, O Brahma, I did not preach amongst men this glorious and excellent Dhamma."*
>
> *The delighted Brahma, thinking - "I made myself the occasion for the Blessed One to expound the Dhamma," respectfully saluted Him and straightaway disappeared.*

Respected scholar, Gombrich (2013) advises that it is essential to 'decode' such texts, especially for a western audience who generally would not admit to the validity of such advice coming from gods or devas. Gombrich tackles critique from Buddhist scholars who have questioned how much of the Early Buddhist Texts can be regarded as reliable. Similar to the position taken by Sujato and Brahmali (2015) and by me in this book, Gombrich speaks directly to the reliability of the development of Buddha's educational philosophy, highlighting the similarity between the Buddha as a teacher and what we might experience as educators as we pursue our teaching career saying that:

> *Teachers, unless they are exceptionally stupid, change both their opinions and their way of putting things. That the Buddha varied his way of putting things according to what audience he was addressing is indeed a commonplace of the Buddhist tradition, which attributes*

> *to him supreme "skill in means"; but that tradition would baulk at the idea that he ever changed his mind. However, I am not committed to the tradition; nor do the two kinds of change, in meaning and expression, necessarily show results which the observer can distinguish. It is mainly writing that freezes our past insights for us and so gives our* oeuvre *a certain consistency; even so, I suspect that there can be few university teachers today who have not had the experience of re-reading something they had written long ago and finding it unfamiliar. (Which is more depressing: to find that what we once wrote now seems all wrong, or to find that it contains facts we have forgotten and bright ideas we can no longer remember having thought of?) Thus, as hard-headed historians, we cannot think that over 45 years the Buddha could have been entirely consistent—and especially when we take into account that he could not read over or playback what he had said. If the texts have any valid claim to be the record of so long a preaching career, they cannot be wholly consistent. Indeed, the boot is on the other foot: the texts are too consistent to be a wholly credible record. It is obvious that literary convention and human forgetfulness have contributed to the tendency recalled in my previous paragraph so as to iron out many of the inconsistencies of both message and expression which must have occurred.* (Gombrich, 2013, p. 9)

The final aspect that I would like to discuss is the concept of the Buddha as *Kalyāṇamitta* reliable guide. My observation is that Buddha was a person comparable to a well-regarded adult educator whose explanation of the pathway to achieving specific experiences and spiritual development could be tested by the learner and found to be true or not. The Buddha performed the role of *Kalyāṇamitta* reliable guide by pointing to his established curriculum and giving thousands of lectures over 45 years that spoke to people's interest and confidence in his approach. Continuing the discussion he had with Ānanda about the *Kalyāṇamitta* teacher role (SN 45.2, SuttaCentral, 2020, paras. 3–5), as discussed in the previous section, he goes on to say:

> *When a bhikkhu* monk *has a* Kalyāṇamitta *good friend, a good companion, a good comrade, it is to be expected that he will develop and cultivate the Noble Eightfold Path.*
>
> *"And how, Ānanda, does a bhikkhu who has a good friend, a good companion, a good comrade, develop and cultivate the Noble Eightfold Path? Here, Ānanda, a bhikkhu develops right view, which is based upon seclusion, dispassion, and cessation, maturing in release. He develops right intention ... right speech ... right action ... right livelihood ... right effort ... right mindfulness ... right concentration, which is based upon seclusion, dispassion, and cessation, maturing in release. It is in this way, Ānanda, that a bhikkhu who has a good friend, a good companion, a good comrade, develops and cultivates the Noble Eightfold Path."*
>
> *"By the following method too, Ānanda, it may be understood how the entire holy life is good friendship, good companionship, good comradeship: by relying upon me as a good friend, Ānanda, beings subject to birth are freed from birth; beings subject to aging are freed from aging; beings subject to death are freed from death; beings subject to sorrow, lamentation, pain, displeasure, and despair are freed from sorrow, lamentation, pain, displeasure, and despair. By this method, Ānanda, it may be understood how the entire holy life is good friendship, good companionship, good comradeship."*

1.3 The Buddha's Approach to the Development of Wisdom from 2,500 Years Ago

This introductory chapter has set the scene for exploring the life of the Buddha as a teacher, the development of his teachings, and his teaching approach; the contemporary context of education, where immigrants from may ethnoreligious traditions have established their Buddhism within countries such as multicultural Australia; a discussion of key terms and definitions and an explanation of the use of the Early Buddhist texts, and the use of Sanskrit, Prakrit, Pāḷi, and English; and, introduction to the Buddha as a person, a spiritual archetype, and, the focus of this monograph, as an educational theorist and notable teacher of how humans can develop inner wisdom.

The second chapter provides a more in-depth examination of the Buddha's 45-year education legacy. Examining what we know of teaching and learning at that time, this chapter makes a detailed examination of the emergence of the Buddha's education theory introduced through an overview of the *cattari ariya saccani* Four Noble Truths and the *aṭṭhaṅgika-magga* Noble Eightfold Path from the *Tipitaka* Buddhist Canon, as the *Buddha-Dhamma* core curriculum. This *Buddha-Dhamma* core curriculum and the *Majjhima Patipada* Middle Way approach to teaching provide an outline of the broad canvas of his educational theory.

In Chap. 3, I present historical evidence about aspects of education in the region in northern India where the Buddha spent his teaching life, known as the heartland of Buddhism, and explore the process of generation, codification, and preservation of the *Tipitaka* Buddhist Canon and its dissemination after the passing of the Buddha from its heartland in India. I examine the second wave of adaptations across the Asian region, noting the assimilation of the Buddha's teachings into tribal Indigenous metaphysics, local spiritual customs, and the slow development of the various schools of Buddhist thought, and their teaching and learning styles. I then move to the third period of adaptation globally with Buddhist acclimatisation in the West through formal and informal teaching and learning contexts, through the education work of both Buddhist temples (for both immigrant and local populations) and *Sangha*, with respect to the protection of the Buddhist Canon, the preservation of ethnocultural versions of Buddhism in the western context, and the emergence of uniquely western adaptations through schools, universities, and the personal development movement.

Chap. 4 makes the transition from an emphasis on the broader historical and sociocultural aspects that influenced the educational approach taken by the Buddha towards an examination of the Buddha as an adult educator with a clear pedagogical intent. This chapter will make a close examination of the various pedagogical approaches used by the Buddha that supported his teaching of the *Buddha-Dhamma* core curriculum of the *cattari ariya saccani* Four Noble Truths and the *aṭṭhaṅgikaṃ maggaṃ* Noble Eightfold Path. These approaches include some that would be familiar to the modern reader, some that have fallen out of favour, or some more akin to Indigenous and traditionally-oriented approaches to pedagogy that continue to be employed by teachers.

The final chapter turns to an analysis of the teaching strategies and pedagogical techniques employed by the Buddha to teach the *Buddha-Dhamma* core curriculum of the *cattari ariya saccani* Four Noble Truths and the *aṭṭhaṅgikaṃ maggaṃ* Noble Eightfold Path found in the *Tipitaka* Buddhist Canon (see Appendixes A and C). It will tease out the Buddha's *Majjhima Patipada* Middle Way methods and examine the importance of these for modern education, in particular the experiential element. I will conclude with a discussion of the key elements of the Buddha's education theory, their importance, and relevance for modern education.

References

Suttas

SuttaCentral. (2020). Saṃyutta Nikāya 45.2. *Upaḍḍhasutta* Half the Holy Life. [Bhikkhu Bodhi, Trans.]. Retrieved December 24 2020 from https://suttacentral.net/sn45.2/en/bodhi. The Connected Discourses of the Buddha (Wisdom Publications, 2000). This excerpt from The Connected Discourses of the Buddha by Bhikkhu Bodhi is licensed under a Creative Commons Attribution - Non Commercial - No Derivs 3.0 Unported License. Based on the work Connected Discourses of the Buddha at Wisdom Publications. Permissions beyond the scope of this license may be available at Wisdom Publications. Prepared for SuttaCentral by Blake Walsh.

SuttaCentral. (2020). Saṃyutta Nikāya 56.11. *Dhammacakkappavattanasutta* Setting in Motion the Wheel of the Dhamma. [Bhikkhu Bodhi, Trans.]. Retrieved December 24 2020 from https://suttacentral.net/sn56.11/en/bodhi. The Connected Discourses of the Buddha (Wisdom Publications, 2000). This excerpt from The Connected Discourses of the Buddha by Bhikkhu Bodhi is licensed under a Creative Commons Attribution—Non Commercial—No Derivs 3.0 Unported License. Based on the work Connected Discourses of the Buddha at Wisdom Publications. Permissions beyond the scope of this license may be available at Wisdom Publications. Prepared for SuttaCentral by Blake Walsh.

SuttaCentral. (2020). Saṃyutta Nikāya 22.58. Upayavagga. Sammāsambuddhasutta The Perfectly Enlightened One. [Bhikkhu Bodhi, Trans.]. Retrieved December 24 2020 from https://suttacentral.net/sn22.58/en/bodhi. The Connected Discourses of the Buddha (Wisdom Publications, 2000). This excerpt from The Connected Discourses of the Buddha by Bhikkhu Bodhi is licensed under a Creative Commons Attribution—Non Commercial—No Derivs 3.0 Unported License. Based on the work Connected Discourses of the Buddha at Wisdom Publications. Permissions beyond the scope of this license may be available at Wisdom Publications. Prepared for SuttaCentral by Blake Walsh.

Authored texts

Beare, H., & Slaughter, R. (1993). *Education for the twenty-first century*. Routledge.

Carrithers, M. (1983). *The Buddha (past masters)*. Oxford University Press.

Conze, E. (1957). *Buddhism: Its essence and development*. Ltd: Munshiram Manoharlal Publishers Pvt.

Davids, T. W. R. (1911). *Buddhist India* Kessinger Publishing.

Gombrich, R. F. (2013). *What the Buddha thought*. Equinox Publishing Ltd.

Laumakis, S. J. (2008). *An introduction to Buddhist philosophy*. Cambridge University Press.
Ma Rhea, Z. (2017a). Buddhist pedagogy in teacher education: Cultivating wisdom by skillful means. *Asia-Pacific Journal of Teacher Education, 46*(2), 199–216. doi.org/10.1080/1359866X.2017.1399984.
Ma Rhea, Z. (2017b). *Wisdom, knowledge, and the postmodern University in Thailand*. Palgrave Macmillan. https://doi.org/10.1057/978-1-137-37694-7.
Ma Rhea, Z., & Teasdale, G. R. (2000). A dialogue between the global and the local. In G. R. Teasdale & Z. Ma Rhea (Eds.), *Local knowledge and wisdom in higher education* (pp. 1–14). Pergamon Elsevier.
Narada Maha Thera. (1992). *A manual of Buddhism*. Buddhist Missionary Society. http://www.purifymind.com/ManualBuddhism.htm.
Narada Maha Thera. (2012). *The Buddha and his teachings* (3rd ed.). Buddhist Publications Society.
Smyth, J., Hattam, R., & Lawson, M. (Eds.). (1998). *Schooling for a fair go*. The Federation Press.
Sujato, Bhikkhu & Brahmali, Bhikkhu. (2015). *The authenticity of the early buddhist texts*. Chroniker Press. https://ocbs.org/wp-content/uploads/2015/09/authenticity.pdf.
SuttaCentral. (2020a). *Kalyāṇamitta*. Retrieved December 30, 2020 from SuttaCentral. SuttaCentral, 2020, https://suttacentral.net/define/kalyāṇamitta.
SuttaCentral. (2020b). *Pacceka*. Retrieved December 30, 2020 from SuttaCentral. https://suttacentral.net/define/pacceka.
The World Commission on Environment and Development. (1987). *Report of the world commission on environment and development: Our common future* (A/42/427). http://www.un-documents.net/our-common-future.pdf.

Chapter 2
Emergence of Buddha's 45-Year Educational Legacy

Abstract This chapter provides a more in-depth examination of the Buddha's 45-year education legacy. Examining what we know of teaching and learning at that time, this chapter makes a detailed examination of the emergence of the Buddha's education theory introduced through an overview of the *cattari ariya saccani* Four Noble Truths and the *aṭṭhaṅgika-magga* Noble Eightfold Path from the *Tipitaka* Buddhist Canon, as the *Buddha-Dhamma* core curriculum. This *Buddha-Dhamma* core curriculum and the *Majjhima Patipada* Middle Way approach to teaching provide an outline of the broad canvas of his educational theory.

Keywords *cattari ariya saccani* Four Noble Truths · *aṭṭhaṅgika-magga* Noble Eightfold Path · *Tipitaka* Buddhist Canon · *Buddha-Dhamma* core curriculum · *Majjhima Patipada* Middle Way · Teaching and learning · Curriculum · Pedagogy

2.1 Aspects Shaping Teaching and Learning in the Time of the Buddha

While this monograph examines the development of inner wisdom through the teachings of the Buddha over 2,500 years ago, there remain communities of people in this contemporary era who maintain and preserve ideas about the teaching and learning of wisdom that have resonance with the earlier times. Interestingly, and something that will be examined more closely in Chap. 3, the ideas of the Buddha have been finding fertile soil across the planet, spreading and settling as they met the cultures of myriad Indigenous peoples and all sorts of other religions and spiritual practices and socio-economic contexts and there remain some enduring features of his approach to teaching and learning that were highly adaptable to each context, successfully enabling a diversity of people to become interested in his ideas, to receive some teachings, to practice according to the teachings, and to walk the pathway towards the development of inner wisdom he had elucidated.

In order to understand some of these contemporary resonances, it is necessary to establish some of the elements of the socio-historical context into which the Buddha was born and through which he taught for 45 years. Scholars have reflected that it

Z. M. Diamond, *Gautama Buddha*, https://doi.org/10.1007/978-981-16-1765-2_2

was a time of significant change (Davids, 1911; Gombrich, 2012; Krishnan, 2008; Sujato & Brahmali, 2015). As Laumakis (2008) describes: 'His was a time when the certainties of traditional ways of thinking and living were being challenged by … the breakdown of tribal federations and the development of powerful monarchies and emerging urban centres' (p. 23). As was discussed in Chap. 1, the Buddha would have been educated in a manner that was typical of his time. He may have undergone teaching in the Brahmanical tradition, and possibly even been trained in warfare as the son of an important clan chief. There are many ways of explaining the context of the Buddha's upbringing but without reliable historical records, it is only possible to offer some possibilities of ideas that may have shaped his eventual development into a world-influencing educator. Certainly, many stories have been told of his protected early upbringing with his parents not wanting to expose him to the cruelties and injustices of the world, that he was of a wealthy and princely caste and had every luxury at his command, and many such elaborations. If one considers the context of his times, and the decisions he went on to make about how to live his life, it is not necessary to believe any of these conjectures to understand his core teachings.

2.1.1 Influence of Early Brahminical Education

Choudhary (2008), Ghosh (2001), and Guruge (2003) provide insight into the Brahminical education that the Buddha would have been privy to, if not educated in. Brahminical education developed in the Vedic period. As Choudhary (2008) explains, Brahminical education in the *Rig Veda* was concerned with the preservation of sacred hymns, passed down orally, concerning cosmology and praising deities, philosophical or speculative questions, virtues, and other metaphysical issues in their hymns. The main body of the *Rig Veda* is the *Samhita* that contains the hymns to the deities. It is the oldest part of the *Rig Veda.* The other three parts are the *Brahmanas,* commentaries on the hymns, the *Aranyakas,* books that delved into the deeper meaning of rituals, and the *Upanishads,* the most recent of the sections of the *Rig Veda.* Phillips (2009) suggests that the early parts of the *Upanishads*, the *Brhadaranyaka, Chandogya, Isha, Taittiriya, Aitareya, Kena, Katha, Mundaka, and Prasna Upanishads* are all pre-Buddhist and pre-Jain, while *Svetasvatara* and *Mandukya* overlap with the earliest Buddhist and Jain literature. Similar to the Buddhist Canon, the *Tipitaka,* the *Rig Vedic* body of knowledge was probably first written down about the third-century BCE (Sujato & Brahmali, 2015; West, 2010). As such, I would suggest that the young Siddhārtha Gautama would have been aware of such methods of spiritual training using the oral transmission method to support accurate memorisation and reproduction of a large body of knowledge.

A *rishi* teacher, having undergone many years of memorisation and verbal transmission of the *Rig Veda,* would have students living in his home to undergo the same training that he had undergone. This would have included those parts of the *Rig Veda* that had been taught to that *rishi.* There were strands and schools of teaching and, as a consequence, not all teachers would have been taught all aspects of the complete

Rig Veda. We do not know if the Buddha was educated at home (normally undertaken in the first *Ashrama* period of life from 0 to 25 when such learning and preparation for life took place) or, like most other students, undertook some sort of initiation ceremony and left home for study. He may also have taken part in debating circles and *parishads* where students discussed various aspects of knowledge. He may also, in his young life, attended conferences summoned by kings in which the representatives of various schools participated. Certainly, in his later life he was invited as a speaker to such conferences.

Gombrich (2012) observes that the Buddha's approach to the preservation of the Buddhist Canon had before it the example of preservation of the *Rig Veda*, 'achieved by dint of a system of extraordinarily long and tedious compulsory education for brahmin boys' (p. 6). Notably, unlike the students who memorised these long *Rig Vedic* texts whose training had started at birth, the people who memorised and codified the Buddha's teachings, the *Sangha*, began their memorisation work in adulthood with many not having the benefit of early training in memorisation. As Gombrich (2012, pp. 6–7) explains, this 'must have required a vast amount of sustained and highly organised effort. Though there is evidence that extraordinary feats of memory are possible for individuals, whether or not they live in pre-literate civilisations, these Buddhist texts amount to hundreds of thousands of lines, so much that only a very few individuals of exceptional mnemonic gifts can ever have mastered the lot'.

2.1.2 *Tribal Roots of Buddhism and Buddha's Pedagogy*

While the Brahminical influences on Buddhism and Jainism, another traditional of spiritual development that arose contemporaneously with the ideas of the Buddha, are important to recognise, there were also other factors that contribute to explaining the profound effect that the Buddha's teachings and the way he taught had on the people of the north-eastern region of India in the fifth century BCE. Rhys Davids, in 1911, made the observation that the 'brahmin books convey the impression that the only recognised, and in fact universally prevalent form of government was that of kings under the guidance and tutelage of priests' (p. 2). Here he makes the argument that there were other established and emerging traditions of education and development co-existing with the emphasis on Brahminical education and its sacrifices. This is an important point with respect to my discussion about the teaching and learning ideas of the Buddha because it is a common belief in modern India that Buddhist ideas are a minor tributary of the great river of the *Rig Veda*, of the Brahmanical traditions, and of contemporary Hinduism. Hence, the argument goes, that the ideas are neither unique nor particularly significant. I do not hold this view.

This monograph makes an argument for the significance of the Buddha as an educator who was teaching during a period of great upheaval in social conditions, where tribal peoples lived in relative independence. As mentioned in Chap. 1, the Buddha's clan, the *Śākya* clan, were a tribal people. Tradition suggests that there were about one million people living in a predominantly settled agricultural community with a number of market towns (Buddhaghosa, cited in Davids, 1911, pp. 18–19). Various of the Buddha's relatives were chiefs during his lifetime, including his father. Their clan territory is estimated to have been about 'fifty miles from east to west and thirty to forty miles southward from the foot of the Himalaya Hills' (Davids, 1911, p. 18) with the administrative centre being Kapilavastu. Rhys Davids also makes the conjecture that there would have been Brahmin priests living in every village, 'whose services were in request at every domestic event' (p. 19). Important for this discussion, beyond historical interest, is the parallel I find between Rhys Davids' account of the socio-economic organisation of the *Śākya* clan and contemporary agrarian and Indigenous communities in the present era. The fact that the *Śākya* clan was an Indigenous people, a 'free republic', drawn into the sphere of emerging kingdoms, places the Buddha in a unique position of understanding tribal Indigenous socio-political and economic freedoms together with his ability to engage with the business of the emerging monarchical and merchant classes in a uniquely democratic manner.

A significant aspect of this democratic tendency of the Buddha was that, contrary to contemporary belief, the Indian caste system was still forming and the Buddha taught his ideas to people of all social positions and occupations. This is a signature of his appeal and how he was able to bridge the spiritual and secular in his programme of education of the people. In Chap. 3 (this edition), such a unique foundation would have profound impact on the ability of the Buddha's ideas to find fertile soil. His teachings came as much from his Indigenous, tribal roots as they did from his exposure to Brahmanical education and tribal socialisation. The following example from the *Janavasabhasutta* (DN 18, SuttaCentral, 2020, paras. 1–8) provides some insight into the extent of his connection with members of other tribal 'free republics' and his assessment of their members in terms of what they had achieved during their lives in spiritual development, an aspect of teaching and learning that has fallen away in contemporary assessment practices:

> *Thus, have I heard.*
>
> *The Exalted One was once staying in Nādika, at the Brick House. Now at that time the Exalted One was wont to make declarations as to the rebirths of such followers (of the doctrine) as had passed away in death among the tribes round about on every side—among the Kāsis and Kosalans, the Vajjians and Mallas, the Chetis and Vaṃsas, the Kurus and Pañcālas, the Macchas and Sūrasenas—saying: 'Such a one has been reborn there, and such a one there.'*
>
> *When the devotees of Nādika heard about the Buddha's answers to those questions, they were uplifted and overjoyed, full of rapture and happiness.*
>
> *Venerable Ānanda heard of the Buddha's statements and the Nādikans' happiness.*

2.2 The Profound Influence of Wandering and Teaching

A signature feature of the Buddha's teaching life, and of central interest to educators, is that the Buddha was a wandering mendicant. He disavowed using vehicles and would not use beasts to carry him. His way of being a teacher was shaped by a daily walking and begging practice. Sometimes he would remain in a village over days or even weeks, relying on people to feed and clothe him. He also needed a place for his ablutions and for him to sleep and teach. In towns and villages where he was supported by clan chiefs and kings, it was easier for him to have sufficient alms-food for the day, and be given an area of forest or grove to sleep, teach, and bathe. In other places such as Madhurā, he was given less food and found the village to be less able to meet his daily needs. As will be discussed more fully in Chap. 5, this was an embodied pedagogy—he literally 'walked his talk' using walking and the practice of asking for food to sharpen and focus his ideas as he learned to teach his 'core curriculum' day by day. He mostly lived and taught outdoors or sometimes under roofed pavilions with no walls. These aspects of his daily teaching life are quite distinct from the modern school environment where teachers struggle to be allowed to teach outdoors or teach students through embodied practices. These differences will prove important as we consider how to approach the education ideas of the Buddhas in the twenty-first-century classroom.

The walking life of the Buddha was familiar to that of other spiritual teachers of that era, called *Paribbajakas.* Law (1918, p. 399), in 'A Short Account of the Wandering Teachers at the Time of the Buddha', says:

> *At the time of the rise of Buddhism there were various classes of wanderers who, in the language of Dr Rhys Davids, 'were teachers or sophists who spent eight or nine months of every year wandering about precisely with the object of engaging in conversational discussions on matters of ethics and philosophy, nature lore and mysticism'. Like the sophists among the Greeks, they differed very much in intelligence, in earnestness and in honesty.*

I examined this aspect of his life more fully (Ma Rhea, 2010) and found it useful that Law (1918) separates two classes of *Paribbajakas* into the *Annatitthiya Paribbajaka*, and the *Brahmina Paribbajaka.* The *Brahmina Paribbajakas*, of the tradition of Brahminical Education, were in the habit of discussing matters relating to this phenomenal world, the term corresponding in some way or other to the ways of life or mundane affairs. The *Annatitthiya Paribbajakas* were interested generally in the question of self-realisation in thought and in conduct, that is to say, in solemn judgements about human life and the whole of things. Similar t o he Buddha, the *Paribbajaka* would shave his head, clothe himself with one piece of cloth or antelope skin or cover his body with grass plucked by cows. He would sleep on bare ground. Law (1918) observes that it is generally believed that wanderers were not known much before the rise of Buddhism.

The Buddha distinguished himself by his ideas. He was not pursuing an extreme form of ascetism through his walking and begging. His was a 'Middle Way' teaching. He was not trying to prove he was more spiritually advanced through the extreme practices that others adopted to attract followers. Rather, he seemed comfortable to live the wandering begging life as a way of getting from place to place and receiving the necessary things to sustain life while he focused on teaching people what he had learned as a reliable path to wisdom.

2.3 What Was Spiritual Development in This Context?

Foundational elements of the Buddha's teachings provided clear guidance to people about their lives, focusing on the development of *pañña* wisdom and *karuṇā* compassion. *Pañña* wisdom is the outcome of a person penetrating the nature of reality. *Karuṇā* compassion, also translated as wise empathy, is one of the *brahmavihāras or the Four Divine Abodes* that, together with compassion provide the emotionally mature ground in which to develop wisdom. The other are *mettā* loving kindness, *muditā* altruistic joy, and *upekkhā* equanimity. Here the Buddha, as an exemplar of both the style of teaching and its content, describes the importance of developing *pañña* wisdom and *karuṇā* compassion as a unified teaching in the *Karuṇāsutta* (SN 46.63, SuttaCentral, 2020, paras. 1–16):

> *Thus, have I heard:*
>
> *Once the Exalted One was staying near Sāvatthī. Then the Exalted One addressed the monks, saying: "Monks."*
>
> *"Yes, lord," replied those monks to the Exalted One. The Exalted One said:*
>
> *"Monks, the idea of compassion, if cultivated and made much of, is of great fruit and great profit. And how cultivated and made much of is the idea of compassion of great fruit and great profit?"*
>
> *"Herein a monk cultivates the limb of wisdom that is* ***mindfulness****, accompanied by the idea of compassion, which is based on seclusion, on dispassion, on cessation, which ends in self-surrender."*
>
> *"He cultivates the limb of wisdom that is investigation of the* ***Norm****, accompanied by the idea of compassion, which is based on seclusion, on dispassion, on cessation, which ends in self-surrender."*
>
> *"He cultivates the limb of wisdom that is* ***energy,*** *..."*
>
> *"He cultivates the limb of wisdom that is* ***zest,*** *...."*
>
> *"He cultivates the limb of wisdom that is* ***tranquillity,*** *..."*
>
> *"He cultivates the limb of wisdom that is* ***concentration,*** *..."*
>
> *"He cultivates the limb of wisdom that is* ***equanimity,*** *..."*
>
> *"Thus cultivated, monks, thus made much of, the idea of compassion is of great fruit and great profit."*

There are a number of features in the above exemplar that are worth noting. Here we find the usual opening lines: 'Thus, I have heard'. This emphasises that the teaching of the Buddha has been memorised and retold by one of the monks. It locates the teaching as being given near Sāvatthī, the capital town of Kosala in India and one of the six great Indian cities during the lifetime of the Buddha. The Kingdom of Kosala was one of the emerging monarchies governed by King Pasenadi, who became a great supporter of the Buddha.

The Buddha passed the greater part of his monastic life in Sāvatthī. It is said that he spent twenty-five rainy seasons in the city, nineteen of them in Jetavana and six in the Pubbarama. Outside the city gate of Sāvatthī was a fishermen's village of five hundred families. Here we see an example of the context of the Buddha's words, in a familiar place where the Buddha's teachings could speak to the merchants of Kosala, the fishermen and their families and to the King.

In this *Sutta*, we can also see the pedagogical format of question and answer used in the Buddha's exposition, where he gives a step-by-step scaffolded answer introducing one new concept [in **bold** for ease of understanding] within a sentence formula that is repeated. All of these sub-concepts (e.g. mindfulness, equanimity and so on) are investigated through the lens of *karuṇā* compassion as part of a holistic approach to the development of *pañña* wisdom. Each concept was grounded in the *Majjhima Patipada* Middle Way path, known as the *aṭṭhaṅgikaṃ maggaṃ* Noble Eightfold Path (see Appendices A & C). The overarching term *sikkhā* describes the training that people followed the *aṭṭhaṅgikaṃ maggaṃ* Noble Eightfold Path recorded in the Early Buddhist Texts. The three domains of knowledge that are practised in this approach are *sīla* morality, *samādhi* concentration, and *vipassanā* insight leading to the development of *pañña* wisdom (Ma Rhea, 2013; Ven Nyanatiloka, 1988).

The concepts introduced above would have been familiar to the people who came to hear the Buddha teach, especially as he returned to places such as Sāvatthī many times to repeat these teachings. Indeed, there were other wandering mendicants and established Brahmin priests of various spiritual traditions teaching in that region of India. There are records of many lively debates and discussions among them in front of interested audiences. But what I see emerging in my analysis is that the Buddha has a disciplined approach to the development of wisdom that is accessible to everyone who is willing to listen, practice, and explore the deeper meaning of the teachings. The layers of meaning are more deeply understood over time and with practice, something that remains central to formal and informal education pedagogy into the contemporary era. This is in sharp contrast to access to some Indigenous and traditional esoteric, metaphysical, and spiritual knowledge that was only revealed after careful assessment of past learning and sometimes higher levels of initiation. The revolution of the Buddha's approach was that when the learner apprehended for him or herself the deeper meaning of teachings through living ethically, practising meditation, and applying discernment to the arising knowledge from practice, the new step on the path would reveal itself. Many people achieved *nibbāna* enlightenment, the complete expression of *pañña* wisdom under the Buddha's guidance, and continue to do so into the present time following the same *aṭṭhaṅgikaṃ maggaṃ* Noble Eightfold Path (see Appendix C).

2.4 The Philosophical Foundation of the Buddha's Education Theory

The discussion in the previous section indicates that during the time of the Buddha, over his teaching career of 45 years, he developed a theory of education of similar import to those great Western philosophers of education about whom we know far more—Socrates, Plato, Aristotle, Augustine, Aquinas, Maimonides, Descartes,

Hobbes, Spinoza, Locke, and Rousseau and more recent education theorists such as Dewey (see, e.g., Rorty, 1998). The education systems of Hinduism, Judaism, and more recent Christianity and Islam, all share the feature with Western theories of education of having been written down. Their ancient pedagogical roots go further back into Indigenous and other traditionally-oriented approaches to education passed on orally to the present day. All education theories are embedded in the preoccupation of how best to educate the young members of a clan, republic, or state to produce its best humans of the future.

The Buddha's approach has an underpinning theory of education that focuses firmly on the development of worldly and transcendental *pañña* wisdom as the goal of education, designed for the 'here and now' and the possibility of achieving *nibbāna* enlightenment in this life or a future rebirth. As such, his teachings are embedded in Indigenous and traditionally-orientated methods. The preservation of his educational philosophy benefitted from notable memorisation efforts until his ideas could be recorded in written forms. This work has enabled a new examination of his theory of education 2,500 after his career ended. The next section provides a brief overview of the *cattari ariya saccani* Four Noble Truths and the *aṭṭhaṅgikaṃ maggaṃ* Noble Eightfold Path.

2.4.1 Understanding the Buddha's Key Educational Ideas

The educational ideas of the Buddha were unique for their time. Indeed, there were aspects of society, environment, and education that influenced the development of the Buddha as a young person but as he reached his maturity, he branched out on his own to find answers that others were unable to give him about the meaning of life and the purpose of education. Over 45 years, he developed and refined the communication of his ideas. These were collected and organised, first orally, and later were written down in a collection of books known as the *Tipitaka* Buddhist Canon containing the *Vinaya, Sutta Pitaka, and Abhidhamma Pitaka.* In this monograph, I mainly focus on the Early Buddhist Texts (EBTs) preserved in the *Sutta Pitaka*, one of the three baskets. The *Suttas* contain the pedagogical approach and core curriculum of teachings that provide the foundation for teaching and learning into the modern era, first collected and taught in nascent universities such as Nalanda, then shared across Asia east and west as far as Greece and Indonesia. Versions of these teachings are found across the world, mostly preserved by monks and nuns of the various Buddhist traditions and taught in temples. Rarer but becoming more common, it is now possible to find schools and universities being established once again in the tradition of Nalanda to embed Buddhist education theories and ideas into the modern formal education system.

During the Buddha's life, he established an approach that is known as *Majjhima Patipada* Middle Way is a holistic approach that balances the development of *sila* moral/ethical, *vipassana* insight/critical thinking, and *samadhi* concentration practices, emphasising the importance of finding the balance between them to experience the emergence of *pañña* wisdom. The *Majjhima Patipada* Middle Way is about finding avoidance of extremes. Finding balance is the crucial element of his teaching arising from his turning away from indulgence in worldly pursuits and extreme ascetic practices. He had experienced both and found neither to be satisfying or leading to wisdom. A discussion of his pedagogy of the *Majjhima Patipada* Middle Way will be undertaken in Chap. 4. In this following section, I will introduce the *Buddha-Dhamma* core curriculum of the *cattari ariya saccani* Four Noble Truths and the *aṭṭhaṅgikaṃ maggaṃ* Noble Eightfold Path, as the philosophical foundations for his education theory, as a teaching approach that leads to the student learning how to avoid extremes and experience the emergence of wisdom. The Buddha's education idea and, arguably, the reason for his approach, is to teach in such a way as to lead the learner to deliverance from what he calls *dukkha* suffering, a word that encompasses all the discontents and dissatisfactions that arise from being human towards a deep inner, satisfying wisdom. Here I will introduce the overall framework, and in the following chapters, I will draw on aspects of this curriculum to establish the importance of these ideas for contemporary education.

The Buddha teaching did what is called 'Setting in Motion the Wheel of the Dhamma'. This teaching is an oft-quoted and studied *Sutta*, the *Dhammacakkappavattanasutta* (SN 56.11, SuttaCentral, 2020, paras. 1–3).

> *Thus, have I heard. On one occasion the Blessed One was dwelling at Bārāṇasī in the Deer Park at Isipatana. There the Blessed One addressed the bhikkhus of the group of five thus:*
>
> *"Bhikkhus, these two extremes should not be followed by one who has gone forth into homelessness. What two? The pursuit of sensual happiness in sensual pleasures, which is low, vulgar, the way of worldlings, ignoble, unbeneficial; and the pursuit of self-mortification, which is painful, ignoble, unbeneficial. Without veering towards either of these extremes, the Tathagata has awakened to the middle way, which gives rise to vision, which gives rise to knowledge, which leads to peace, to direct knowledge, to enlightenment, to Nibbāna."*
>
> *"And what, bhikkhus, is that middle way awakened to by the Tathagata, which gives rise to vision … which leads to Nibbāna? It is this Noble Eightfold Path; that is, right view, right intention, right speech, right action, right livelihood, right effort, right mindfulness, right concentration. This, bhikkhus, is that middle way awakened to by the Tathagata, which gives rise to vision, which gives rise to knowledge, which leads to peace, to direct knowledge, to enlightenment, to Nibbāna."*

In the *Khandhasutta* (SN 56.13, SuttaCentral, 2020, para. 1), the Buddha introduces a succinct overview to his audience, saying:

> *"Bhikkhus, there are these Four Noble Truths. What four? The noble truth of suffering, the noble truth of the origin of suffering, the noble truth of the cessation of suffering, the noble truth of the way leading to the cessation of suffering."*

He then goes on to expound the four aspects individually. For each of the *cattari ariya saccani* Four Noble Truths, I will give its name, the direct explanation given by the Buddha and an example of an elaboration given by him in one of his many teachings about this aspect. For the reader who is unfamiliar with these ideas, I have tried to provide enough textual information from the Early Buddhist Texts to examine and reflect on his ideas, given their philosophically foundational importance in developing an understanding of his contribution to education. He begins with *dukkha ariya sacca* the First Noble Truth (SN 56.13, SuttaCentral, 2020, para. 2):

"And what, bhikkhus, is the noble truth of suffering? It should be said: the five aggregates subject to clinging; that is, the form aggregate subject to clinging ... the consciousness aggregate subject to clinging. This is called the noble truth of suffering."

The *dukkha ariya sacca* First Noble Truth asks the learner to contemplate that the individual is only a combination of ever-changing physical or mental forces made up of the 5 aggregates.

He continues with *dukkha samudaya ariya sacca* the Second Noble Truth (SN 56.13, SuttaCentral, 2020, para. 3):

"And what, bhikkhus, is the noble truth of the origin of suffering? It is this craving which leads to renewed existence, accompanied by delight and lust, seeking delight here and there; that is, craving for sensual pleasures, craving for existence, craving for extermination. This is called the noble truth of the origin of suffering."

He often explains that *dukkha* is, of itself, not an originary cause as others were teaching at the time, correcting Bhikkhu Sāti on this point, for example, on one occasion when the Buddha was living at Sāvatthī in Jeta's Grove, Anāthapiṇḍika's Park. He explains to Sāti in the *Mahātaṇhāsaṅkhayasutta* (MN 38, SuttaCentral, 2020, para. 29):

"So, bhikkhus, with ignorance as condition, formations come to be; with formations as condition, consciousness; with consciousness as condition, mentality-materiality; with mentality-materiality as condition, the sixfold base; with the sixfold base as condition, contact; with contact as condition, feeling; with feeling as condition, craving; with craving as condition, clinging; with clinging as condition, being; with being as condition, birth; with birth as condition, ageing and death, sorrow, lamentation, pain, grief, and despair come to be. Such is the origin of this whole mass of suffering."

Continuing with *dukkha nirodho ariya sacca* The Third Noble Truth (SN 56.13, SuttaCentral, 2020, para. 4):

"And what, bhikkhus, is the noble truth of the cessation of suffering? It is the remainderless fading away and cessation of that same craving, the giving up and relinquishing of it, freedom from it, nonreliance on it. This is called the noble truth of the cessation of suffering."

In this Truth, he elaborates his idea of causation in the *Paṭiccasamuppādasutta* (SN 12.1, SuttaCentral, 2020, paras. 1–4), where he explains how suffering arises and how everything is *aññamañña paccayo* interdependent and mutually arising in a significant teaching on dependent origination, saying:

Thus, have I heard. On one occasion the Blessed One was dwelling at Sāvatthī in Jeta's Grove, Anāthapiṇḍika's Park. There the Blessed One addressed the bhikkhus thus: "Bhikkhus!"

"Venerable sir!" those bhikkhus replied. The Blessed One said this:

"Bhikkhus, I will teach you dependent origination. Listen to that and attend closely, I will speak."

"Yes, venerable sir," those bhikkhus replied. The Blessed One said this:

"And what, bhikkhus, is dependent origination? With ignorance as condition, volitional formations come to be; with volitional formations as condition, consciousness; with consciousness as condition, name-and-form; with name-and-form as condition, the six sense bases; with the six sense bases as condition, contact; with contact as condition, feeling; with

> *feeling as condition, craving; with craving as condition, clinging; with clinging as condition, existence; with existence as condition, birth; with birth as condition, aging-and-death, sorrow, lamentation, pain, displeasure, and despair come to be. Such is the origin of this whole mass of suffering. This, bhikkhus, is called dependent origination".*

This is a very important foundation for his theory of education because he targets ignorance as an arising condition of *dukkha* suffering, proposing that with a clear understanding of suffering, and having the arising desire to resolve suffering in one's life, the learner begins to think about thoughts and actions differently. The Buddha's theory of causation has twelve links of dependent origination, where he shows the origin and cessation of suffering dependent on ignorance. In the next section of this teaching, he then explains the pathway to the cessation of suffering (SN 12.1, SuttaCentral, 2020, para. 5) explaining:

> *"But with the remainderless fading away and cessation of ignorance comes cessation of volitional formations; with the cessation of volitional formations, cessation of consciousness; with the cessation of consciousness, cessation of name-and-form; with the cessation of name-and-form, cessation of the six sense bases; with the cessation of the six sense bases, cessation of contact; with the cessation of contact, cessation of feeling; with the cessation of feeling, cessation of craving; with the cessation of craving, cessation of clinging; with the cessation of clinging, cessation of existence; with the cessation of existence, cessation of birth; with the cessation of birth, aging-and-death, sorrow, lamentation, pain, displeasure, and despair cease. Such is the cessation of this whole mass of suffering."*

These are examples of an extensive body of work that, taken together, move back and forth in explanation and refinement of the second and third Noble Truths. In this short monograph, it is not possible to provide the full extent of the teachings but to point to their central importance in his education philosophy. As it is explained, 'the *Nidāna Saṃyutta* Linked Discourses on Causation is a major collection containing 93 discourses on the core Buddhist teaching of dependent origination. Dependent origination presents a series of conditional links laying bare how suffering originates and how it ends'. Importantly, as is explained (SN 12, SuttaCentral, 2020)[1]:

> *It integrates psychological and existential aspects of suffering, showing how when bound by attachment we make choices that bind us to transmigrating into future lives. One of the core purposes is to explain how rebirth takes place without having to invoke metaphysical concepts such as a 'soul'.*

For the Buddha, this endless round of arising and ceasing is the cause of everything that comes into being. He explains (SN 12.23, SuttaCentral, 2020, para. 21):

> *"Just as, bhikkhus, when rain pours down in thick droplets on a mountain top, the water flows down along the slope and fills the cleft, gullies, and creeks; these being full fill up the pools; these being full fill up the lakes; these being full fill up the streams; these being full fill up the rivers; and these being full fill up the great ocean."*

In the Fourth Noble Truth, he reveals the *dukkha nirodha gamini patipada ariya sacca* path that provides the framework to enable his educational philosophy's gradual teaching. It is, importantly, a practice pathway rather than something that

[1] See expanded description under the *Nidāna Saṃyutta* tab (https://suttacentral.net/sn12).

can be apprehended simply by having book knowledge of it. He says (SN 56.13, SuttaCentral, 2020, para. 5):

> *"And what, bhikkhus, is the noble truth of the way leading to the cessation of suffering? It is this Noble Eightfold Path; that is, right view, right thought, right speech, right action, right livelihood, right effort, right mindfulness, and right concentration. This is called the noble truth of the way leading to the cessation of suffering."*

As is explained (SuttaCentral, 2020), the *Saṃyutta Nikaya* Linked Discourses on the Truths contains 131 discourses on the *cattari ariya saccani* Four Noble Truths: suffering, its origin, its cessation, and the path. In the *dukkha nirodha gamini patipada ariya sacca* Fourth Noble Truth, the Buddha lays out the steps in the process by which a learner cultivates wisdom over time, gradually, and by experience (SN 56.13, SuttaCentral, 2020). The wisdom being sought is emergent through practising the teachings associated with each step. In modern educational terms, this is scaffolded, developmental learning that is guided and inquiry-based.

The *Mahāvaggasaṃyutta* Great Book consists of twelve saṁyuttas, almost all of which deal with an aspect of Buddhist practice, or the path. As the authors of the explanations at SuttaCentral explain, 'This book is the primary source for these teachings' (SN, Mahāvaggasaṃyutta, SuttaCentral, 2020).[2] The key teachings are found in the *Magga Saṃyutta* Linked Discourses on the Path contains 180 discourses on the *aṭṭhaṅgikaṃ maggaṃ* Noble Eightfold Path, which gives rise to a curriculum of study and practice known as the *Majjhima Patipada* Middle Way. Buddhist scholars (SN, Magga Saṃyutta, SuttaCentral, 2020)[3] suggest that this body of teachings 'is the first and most important of all the Buddha's teachings on the path of spiritual practice'. The Buddha explains the path in this way (SN 45.1, SuttaCentral, 2020, paras. 1–4):

> *Thus have I heard. On one occasion the Blessed One was dwelling at Sāvatthī in Jeta's Grove, Anāthapiṇḍika's Park. There the Blessed One addressed the bhikkhus thus: "Bhikkhus!"*
>
> *"Venerable sir!" those bhikkhus replied. The Blessed One said this:*
>
> *"Bhikkhus, ignorance is the forerunner in the entry upon unwholesome states, with shamelessness and fearlessness of wrongdoing following along. For an unwise person immersed in ignorance, wrong view springs up. For one of wrong view, wrong intention springs up. For one of wrong intention, wrong speech springs up. For one of wrong speech, wrong action springs up. For one of wrong action, wrong livelihood springs up. For one of wrong livelihood, wrong effort springs up. For one of wrong effort, wrong mindfulness springs up. For one of wrong mindfulness, wrong concentration springs up."*
>
> *"Bhikkhus, true knowledge is the forerunner in the entry upon wholesome states, with a sense of shame and fear of wrongdoing following along. For a wise person who has arrived at true knowledge, right view springs up. For one of right view, right intention springs up. For one of right intention, right speech springs up. For one of right speech, right action springs up. For one of right action, right livelihood springs up. For one of right livelihood, right effort springs up. For one of right effort, right mindfulness springs up. For one of right mindfulness, right concentration springs up."*

---

[2]See expanded description under the *Mahāvaggasaṃyutta* tab (https://suttacentral.net/sn-mahavaggasamyutta).

[3]See expanded description under the *Magga Saṃyutta* tab (https://suttacentral.net/sn-mahavaggasamyutta).

At Sāvatthī, he also gives definitions and analysis for each of these steps on the *aṭṭhaṅgikaṃ maggaṃ* Noble Eightfold Path (SN 45.8, SuttaCentral, 2020, paras. 1–11), recorded succinctly in this way:

> *"Bhikkhus, I will teach you the Noble Eightfold Path and I will analyse it for you. Listen to that and attend closely, I will speak."*
>
> *"Yes, venerable sir," those bhikkhus replied. The Blessed One said this:*
>
> *"And what, bhikkhus, is the Noble Eightfold Path? Right view ... right concentration."*
>
> *"And what, bhikkhus, is right view? Knowledge of suffering, knowledge of the origin of suffering, knowledge of the cessation of suffering, knowledge of the way leading to the cessation of suffering: this is called right view."*
>
> *"And what, bhikkhus, is right intention? Intention of renunciation, intention of non-ill will, intention of harmlessness: this is called right intention."*
>
> *"And what, bhikkhus, is right speech? Abstinence from false speech, abstinence from divisive speech, abstinence from harsh speech, abstinence from idle chatter: this is called right speech."*
>
> *"And what, bhikkhus, is right action? Abstinence from the destruction of life, abstinence from taking what is not given, abstinence from sexual misconduct: this is called right action."*
>
> *"And what, bhikkhus, is right livelihood? Here a noble disciple, having abandoned a wrong mode of livelihood, earns his living by a right livelihood: this is called right livelihood."*
>
> *"And what, bhikkhus, is right effort? Here, bhikkhus, a bhikkhu generates desire for the non-arising of un-arisen evil unwholesome states; he makes an effort, arouses energy, applies his mind, and strives. He generates desire for the abandoning of arisen evil unwholesome states.... He generates desire for the arising of unarisen wholesome states.... He generates desire for the maintenance of arisen wholesome states, for their non-decay, increase, expansion, and fulfilment by development; he makes an effort, arouses energy, applies his mind, and strives. This is called right effort."*
>
> *"And what, bhikkhus is right mindfulness? Here, bhikkhus, a bhikkhu dwells contemplating the body in the body, ardent, clearly comprehending, mindful, having removed covetousness and displeasure in regard to the world. He dwells contemplating feelings in feelings, ardent, clearly comprehending, mindful, having removed covetousness and displeasure in regard to the world. He dwells contemplating mind in mind, ardent, clearly comprehending, mindful, having removed covetousness and displeasure in regard to the world. He dwells contemplating phenomena in phenomena, ardent, clearly comprehending, mindful, having removed covetousness and displeasure in regard to the world. This is called right mindfulness."*
>
> *"And what, bhikkhus, is right concentration? Here, bhikkhus, secluded from sensual pleasures, secluded from unwholesome states, a bhikkhu enters and dwells in the first jhana, which is accompanied by thought and examination, with rapture and happiness born of seclusion. With the subsiding of thought and examination, he enters and dwells in the second jhana, which has internal confidence and unification of mind, is without thought and examination, and has rapture and happiness born of concentration. With the fading away as well of rapture, he dwells equanimous and, mindful and clearly comprehending, he experiences happiness with the body; he enters and dwells in the third jhana of which the noble ones declare: 'He is equanimous, mindful, one who dwells happily.' With the abandoning of pleasure and pain, and with the previous passing away of joy and displeasure, he enters and dwells in the fourth jhana, which is neither painful nor pleasant and includes the purification of mindfulness by equanimity. This is called right concentration."*

I have quoted this text in full to give the reader a sense of the detail provided by the Buddha in his discourses and expositions of his core ideas. He returns to this explanation numerous times and he provides tailored explanations to people depending on their questions, their progress in practising his methods, and in response to what they have experienced. Despite all the variations, he reiterates this core idea so frequently that it forms the basis for his pedagogical approach and the core curriculum, the *Buddha-Dhamma*, that is preserved into the modern era.

In the following chapters, I move to a discussion of how these core teachings and the pedagogy for the gradual *Majjhima Patipada* Middle Way approach were codified through the considerable efforts of the Buddha, the *Sangha*, and myriad followers of all walks of life who took it upon themselves to disseminate these teaching across place and over time, leaving us with a sophisticated and sustainable education philosophy for the development of human wisdom that is teachable into the twenty-first century and beyond.

References

Suttas

SuttaCentral. (2020). Dīgha Nikāya 18. *Janavasabhasutta* With Janavasabha. [Bhikkhu Sujato, Trans.]. Retrieved December 24, 2020, from https://suttacentral.net/dn18/en/sujato. Translated for SuttaCentral by Bhikkhu Sujato, 2018. Dedicated to the public domain via Creative Commons Zero (CC0). You are encouraged to copy, reproduce, adapt, alter, or otherwise make use of this translation in any way you wish. Attribution is appreciated but not legally required.

SuttaCentral. (2020). Majjhima Nikāya 38. *Mahātaṇhāsaṅkhayasutta* The Greater Discourse on the Destruction of Craving. [Bhikku Bodhi, Trans.]. Retrieved December 24, 2020, from https://suttacentral.net/mn38/en/bodhi. The Middle Length Discourses of the Buddha (Wisdom Publications, 2009). This excerpt from The Middle Length Discourses of the Buddha by Bhikkhu Bodhi is licensed under a Creative Commons Attribution—Non Commercial—No Derivs 3.0 Unported License. Based on the work The Middle Length Discourses of the Buddha at Wisdom Publications. Permissions beyond the scope of this license may be available at Wisdom Publications. Prepared for SuttaCentral by Blake Walsh.

SuttaCentral (2020). Saṃyutta Nikāya 12. *Nidāna Saṃyutta*. Retrieved December 24, 2020, from https://suttacentral.net/sn12.

SuttaCentral. (2020). Saṃyutta Nikāya 12.1. *Paṭiccasamuppādasutta* Dependent Origination. [Bhikku Bodhi, Trans.]. Retrieved December 24, 2020, from https://suttacentral.net/sn12.1/en/bodhi. The Connected Discourses of the Buddha (Wisdom Publica-tions, 2000). This excerpt from The Connected Discourses of the Buddha by Bhikkhu Bodhi is licensed under a Creative Commons Attribution—Non Commercial—No Derivs 3.0 Un-ported License. Based on the work Connected Discourses of the Buddha at Wisdom Publications. Permissions beyond the scope of this license may be available at Wisdom Publications. Prepared for SuttaCentral by Blake Walsh.

SuttaCentral. (2020). Saṃyutta Nikāya 12.23. *Upanisasutta* Proximate Cause. [Bhikku Bodhi, Trans.]. Retrieved December 24, 2020, from https://suttacentral.net/sn12.23/en/bodhi. The Connected Discourses of the Buddha (Wisdom Publica-tions, 2000). This excerpt from The Connected Discourses of the Buddha by Bhikkhu Bodhi is li-censed under a Creative Commons Attribution—Non Commercial—No Derivs 3.0 Un-ported License. Based on the work Connected Discourses of the Buddha at Wisdom Publications. Permissions beyond the scope of this license may be available at Wisdom Publications. Prepared for SuttaCentral by Blake Walsh.

SuttaCentral. (2020). Saṃyutta Nikāya 45.1. *Avijjāsutta* Ignorance. [Bhikku Bodhi, Trans.]. Retrieved December 24, 2020, from https://suttacentral.net/sn45.1/en/bodhi. The Connected Discourses of the Buddha (Wisdom Publications, 2000). This excerpt from The Connected Discourses of the Buddha by Bhikkhu Bodhi is licensed under a Creative Commons Attribution—Non Commercial—No Derivs 3.0 Unported License. Based on the work Connected Discourses of the Buddha at Wisdom Publications. Permissions beyond the scope of this license may be available at Wisdom Publications. Prepared for SuttaCentral by Blake Walsh.

SuttaCentral. (2020). Saṃyutta Nikāya 45.8. *Vibhaṅgasutta* Analysis. [Bhikku Bodhi, Trans.]. Retrieved December 24, 2020, from https://suttacentral.net/sn45.8/en/bodhi. The Connected Discourses of the Buddha (Wisdom Publica-tions, 2000). This excerpt from The Connected Discourses of the Buddha by Bhikkhu Bodhi is licensed under a Creative Commons Attribution—Non Commercial—No Derivs 3.0 Un-ported License. Based on the work Connected Discourses of the Buddha at Wisdom Publications. Permissions beyond the scope of this license may be available at Wisdom Publications. Prepared for SuttaCentral by Blake Walsh.

SuttaCentral. (2020). Saṃyutta Nikāya 46.63. *Karuṇāsutta* Compassion. [F. L. Woodward, Trans.]. Retrieved December 24 2020 from https://suttacentral.net/sn46.63/en/woodward. Translated by Frank Lee Woodward. The Pāḷi Text Society Commercial Rights Reserved, Creative Commons Licence. This translation was downloaded on 2017 from http://obo.genaud.net/. HTML editing for SuttaCentral 2017 by Brother Joe Smith AKA Bhikkhu Dhammadāsa.

SuttaCentral. (2020). Saṃyutta Nikāya 56.11. *Dhammacakkappavattanasutta* Setting in Motion the Wheel of the Dhamma. [Bhikku Bodhi, Trans.]. Retrieved December 24, 2020, from https://suttacentral.net/sn56.11/en/bodhi. The Connected Discourses of the Buddha (Wisdom Publications, 2000). This excerpt from The Connected Discourses of the Buddha by Bhikkhu Bodhi is li-censed under a Creative Commons Attribution—Non Commercial—No Derivs 3.0 Unported License. Based on the work Connected Discourses of the Buddha at Wisdom Publications. Permissions beyond the scope of this license may be available at Wisdom Publications. Prepared for SuttaCentral by Blake Walsh.

SuttaCentral. (2020). Saṃyutta Nikāya 56.13. *Khandhasutta* Aggregates. [Bhikku Bodhi, Trans.]. Retrieved December 24, 2020, from https://suttacentral.net/sn56.13/en/bodhi. The Connected Discourses of the Buddha (Wisdom Publications, 2000). This excerpt from The Connected Discourses of the Buddha by Bhikkhu Bodhi is licensed under a Creative Commons Attribution—Non Commercial—No Derivs 3.0 Unported License. Based on the work Connected Discourses of the Buddha at Wisdom Publications. Permissions beyond the scope of this license may be available at Wisdom Publications. Prepared for SuttaCentral by Blake Walsh.

SuttaCentral. (2020). Saṃyutta Nikāya. *Magga Saṃyutta.* Retrieved December 24, 2020, from https://suttacentral.net/sn-mahavaggasamyutta.

SuttaCentral. (2020). Saṃyutta Nikāya. *Mahāvaggasaṃyutta.* Retrieved December 24, 2020, from https://suttacentral.net/sn-mahavaggasamyutta.

Authored Texts

Choudhary, S. K. (2008). Higher education in India: A socio-historical journey from ancient period to 2006–07. *Journal of Educational Enquiry, 8*(1), 50–72. https://ojs.unisa.edu.au/index.php/EDEQ/article/view/484.

Davids, T. W. R. (1911). *Buddhist India.* Kessinger Publishing.

Ghosh, L. (2001). India-Thailand cultural interactions: Glimpses from the past to present. In L. Ghosh (Ed.), *India-Thailand Cultural Interactions: Glimpses from the past to present* (pp. 1–11). Springer Nature Singapore Pte Ltd. https://doi.org/10.1007/978-981-10-3854-9.

Gombrich, R. F. (2012). *Buddhist precept & practice* (1st ed.). Routledge.

Guruge, A. W. P. (2003). How the Buddha taught. *Hsi Lai Journal of Humanistic Buddhism, 4,* 23–53. https://ir.uwest.edu/s/index/item/525.
Krishnan, G. P. (2008). *On the Nalanda trail: Buddhism in India, China, and Southeast Asia.* Asian Civilisations Museum.
Laumakis, S. J. (2008). *An introduction to Buddhist philosophy.* Cambridge University Press.
Law, B. C. (1918). A short account of the wandering teachers at the time of the Buddha. *Journal of the Asiatic Society of Bengal, 14,* 399–406. http://enlight.lib.ntu.edu.tw/FULLTEXT/JR-ENG/lawa.htm.
Ma Rhea, Z. (2010). Transmorphosis: Negotiating discontinuities in academic work. *Policy Futures in Education, 8*(6), 632–643. https://doi.org/10.2304/pfie.2010.8.6.632.
Ma Rhea, Z. (2013). Buddhist wisdom and modernisation: Finding the balance in globalized Thailand. *Globalizations, 10*(4), 635–650. https://doi.org/10.1080/14747731.2013.806739.
Phillips, S. H. (2009). *Yoga, karma, and rebirth: A brief history and philosophy.* Columbia University Press.
Rorty, A. (1998). *Philosophers on education: New historical perspectives* (1st ed.). Routledge. https://doi.org/10.4324/9780203981610.
Sujato, B., & Brahmali, B. (2015). *The authenticity of the early buddhist texts.* Chroniker Press. https://ocbs.org/wp-content/uploads/2015/09/authenticity.pdf.
SuttaCentral. (2020). *Acknowledgements.* Retrieved December 08, 2020, from SuttaCentral. https://suttacentral.net/acknowledgments.
Ven Nyanatiloka. (1988). *Buddhist dictionary: Manual of buddhist terms and doctrine* (4th ed., reprinted). Buddhist Publication Society.
West, B. A. (2010). *Encyclopedia of the peoples of Asia and Oceania.* Facts on File.

Chapter 3
The Buddha's Education Philosophy: From the Heartland

Abstract In this chapter, I present historical evidence about aspects of education in the region in northern India where the Buddha spent his teaching life, known as the heartland of Buddhism, and explore the process of generation, codification, and preservation of the *Tipitaka* Buddhist Canon and its dissemination after the passing of the Buddha from its heartland in India. I examine the second wave of adaptations across the Asian region, noting the assimilation of the Buddha's teachings into tribal Indigenous metaphysics, local spiritual customs, and the slow development of the various schools of Buddhist thought, and their teaching and learning styles. I then move to the third period of adaptation globally with Buddhist acclimatisation in the West through formal and informal teaching and learning contexts, through the education work of both Buddhist temples (for both immigrant and local populations) and Sangha, with respect to the protection of the Buddhist Canon, the preservation of ethnocultural versions of Buddhism in the western context, and the emergence of uniquely western adaptations through schools, universities, and the personal development movement.

Keywords Heartland Buddhism · Asian Buddhism · Theravāda Buddhism · Mahayana Buddhism · Zen Buddhism · Vajrayana Buddhism · Western Buddhism · History of Buddhism

3.1 Introduction

During the 45-year span of the Buddha's teaching life, he spent considerable time teasing out how to teach what he had learnt. At the time, he was recognised as having generated new knowledge, but it was the work of codification of his knowledge into a body of information that was teachable and that, eventually, after his passing, would be disseminated across the globe. His was an experience-based knowledge held tacitly, and in the initial period, known only to him. As was discussed in previous chapters, he was persuaded of his duty to teach what he had come to understand. Influential modern theorist in the sociology of knowledge, Polanyi (1958/1998) might term the experiential knowledge that he held as tacit knowledge. Polanyi recognised that it is not necessarily possible to make all tacit knowledge explicit. His and work

Z. M. Diamond, *Gautama Buddha*, https://doi.org/10.1007/978-981-16-1765-2_3

of those such as Nonaka and Takeuchi (1995) showed that only those aspects of personal knowledge, individually held, that can become explicit knowledge can then be communicated to other people as information sharing. Nonaka and Takeuchi (1995) helpfully describe the nature of this process as being Socialisation, Externalisation, Combination, and Internalisation but employ an important addition to this seemingly linear process, using the metaphor of a spiral to describe their ideas about knowledge creation. The idea of a spiral, now adopted into the lexicon of knowledge management, is useful when considering the process by which people learned the Buddha's ideas, practised them and examined them for their deeper meaning.

The process of communicating tacitly-held knowledge into teachable information has been recognised too by scholars working in the field of Traditional Ecological Knowledge management (Langton & Ma Rhea, 2003; Muecke, 2011; Parsaye & Chignell, 1988). Zeng (2017, p. 78) observes that 'Indigenous traditional knowledge is largely tacit knowledge. However, the tacit knowledge can be captured through three major approaches: interviewing experts, learning by being told, and learning by observation'. Given the rural, tribal context of the Buddha's world and the codification methods of Brahminical education, there is evidence in the Early Buddhist Texts (EBTs; see Chap. 1, this edition) that such socially-constructed, community-based methods of knowledge management were also used to preserve the teachings of the Buddha.

I will employ some of these ideas of Indigenous and corporate knowledge management to describe how the tacit, direct, experiential knowledge of a man living in a rural region of northern India 2500 years ago became explicitly held by him, then codified and transferred across space and time surviving surprisingly intact into the present day. That it may be a remarkable case in successful intergenerational knowledge management is only eclipsed by the efficacy of its teaching methods and the teachability of its core ideas, matters to be discussed in-depth in the following chapters. In this next section, I present historical evidence about aspects of education in the region in northern India, where the Buddha spent his teaching life, known as the heartland.

3.1.1 The Heartland of the Buddha's Teaching Life

Krishnan (2008, p. 19) identifies eight sites in northern India and the southern foothills of Nepal of importance in the Buddha's life: Lumbini, Bodhgaya, Saranath, Kapilavastu, Rajgir, Shravasti, Vaishali, and Kushinagar.[1] I consider these places to encompass what I will term 'heartland Buddhism' (Fig. 3.1).

[1] Ānandajoti Bhikkhu notes that the old names on this map accord to the modern names: Uruvelā = Bodhgaya; Bārāṇasī = Varanasi; Isipatana = Sarnath; Rājagaha = Rajgir; Vesālī = Vaishali; Kapilavatthu = Kapilavastu; Sāvatthī = Shravasti (Ānandajoti Bhikkhu, 2013: https://www.ancient-buddhist-texts.net/Maps/During-Buddhas-Time/Map-02-Early-Career.htm).

Fig. 3.1 Lumbini: UNESCO heritage site (*Note* Adapted from "Lumbini, the birthplace of the Lord Buddha" by UNESCO, 2020. [https://whc.unesco.org/en/list/666/#:~:text=The%20Lord%20Buddha%20was%20born,Emperor%20Asoka%20in%20249%20BC]. Reprinted with permission)

UNESCO confirm the location of the sacred area of Lumbini located in the Terai plains of southern Nepal as being the birthplace of the Buddha, testified by the inscription on the pillar erected by the Mauryan Emperor Asoka in 319 BC. Located on the traditional estates of the *Śākya* clan about 55 km to the east of the large regional town of Kapilavatthu (modern-day Kapilavastu), the country was a republic, governed by a council of chiefs, ruled over by an elected chief.

The Buddha's strong clan connections enabled him to safely walk between other estates and monarchies after proper protocols had been observed. These protocols, rarely highlighted in Buddhist scholarly commentaries, gave the Buddha the necessary permission to undertake his teaching in safety and with respect. Very much present in the *Suttas*, Indigenous echoes of the necessity to follow proper cultural protocols when teaching about Indigenous topics in teacher education, for example, continue into the present. Those charged with memorising the *Suttas*, the *Sangha*, included information at the commencement of each *Sutta* about relevant information such as the clan, the place, any necessary permissions that had been given, and protocols that had been followed. For example (AN 4.183, SuttaCentral, 2020, para. 1):

> *I have heard that on one occasion the Blessed One was staying at Rājagaha in the Bamboo Grove, the Squirrels' Sanctuary. Then Vassakara the brahman, the minister to the king of*

Magadha, approached the Blessed One and, on arrival, exchanged courteous greetings with him. After an exchange of friendly greetings & courtesies, he sat to one side.

In another example, there were established practices for when and how a monk should go out each day, begging for food and then commence his daily meditation safely in an area of the forest where he was allowed to be (SA 236, SuttaCentral, 2020, para. 1):

Thus, have I heard.

At one time the Buddha was staying at Jetavana, Anāthapiṇḍika's park at Śrāvastī. Then, in the morning, the venerable Śāriputra, having put on his outer robe and taken his bowl, went into the town of Śrāvastī for alms-food. Having received alms-food, he returned to the monastery. After putting away his robe and bowl and washing his feet, he took a sitting mat and went into the forest for day-time seated meditation.

The map (Fig. 3.2) depicts the places where the Buddha spent his teaching career, walking between towns, staying for the necessary time and moving on to the next town throughout an annual cycle. According to Ānandajoti Bhikkhu, 'This map represents an area that is approx. 550 km from East to West and 400 km from North to South is approx. 550 km from East to West and 400 km from North to South' (Bhante Ānandajoti, 2012, para. 1).
The westernmost direction of his teaching circuit was Dakkhiṇa-Madhurā (Sujato & Brahmali, 2015, p. 14). The *Madhurāsutta* (AN 5.220, SuttaCentral, 2020, para. 1)

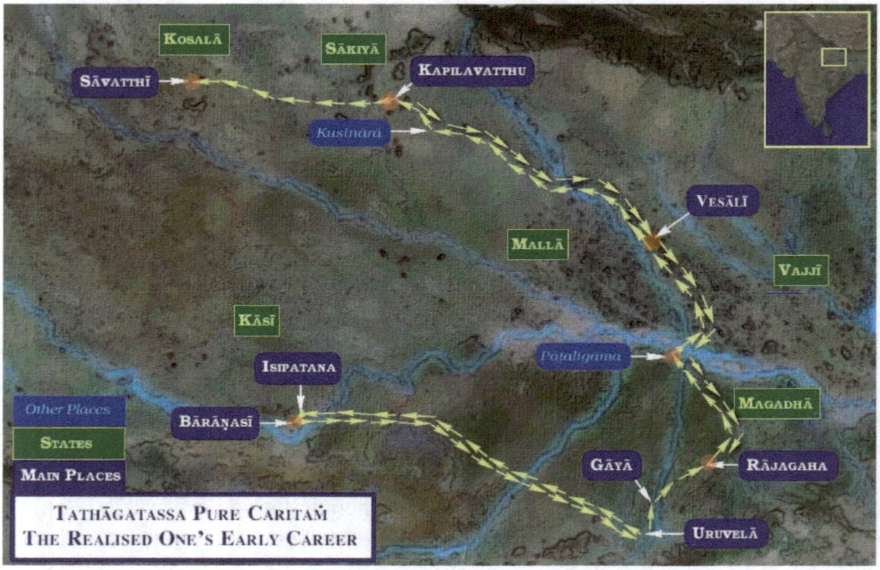

Fig. 3.2 Places where the Buddha spent his teaching career (*Note* Adapted from "The Realised One's early career" by Ānandajoti Bhikkhu, 2012 [https://www.ancient-buddhist-texts.net/Maps/During-Buddhas-Time/Map-02-Early-Career.htm]. Reprinted with permission [Credit Ānandajoti Bhikkhu])

describes that this was a place of drawbacks for the Buddha. It is recorded that he said:

> *"Mendicants, there are these five drawbacks of Madhurā. What five? The ground is uneven and dusty, the dogs are fierce, the native spirits are vicious, and it's hard to get almsfood. These are the five drawbacks of Madhurā."*

Dakkhiṇa-Madhurā was located in the province of modern Uttar Pradesh, the *Paṭhamasaṃvāsasutta* (AN 4.53, SuttaCentral, 2020) records such a journey made by the Buddha in this region. It records that once when the Buddha was journeying from Madhurā to Verañja and stopped under a tree by the wayside, a large number of householders, both men and women, came and listened to him teach. The easternmost place where he taught was Kajaṅgalā, a territory located near Rajmahal in ancient times, in the eastern part of India. (Sujato & Brahmali, 2015, p. 14). Over the 12 months, he normally spent three months of the rainy season in one place, a seasonal time in Asia where travel was difficult, and it became easier for people to feed the Buddha and his monks in one place (Fig. 3.3). This seasonal accommodation has become known as the time of *vassa* 'Rains Retreat', and it has become an established aspect of the annual Buddhist calendar followed across the world by monks and laypeople, regardless of seasonality.
In the *Saṃyutta Nikāya* Linked Discourses, we gain some insight into the process of walking from village to village undertaken by the Buddha, the way that the people learned about his movements throughout the year, and the preparations they made.

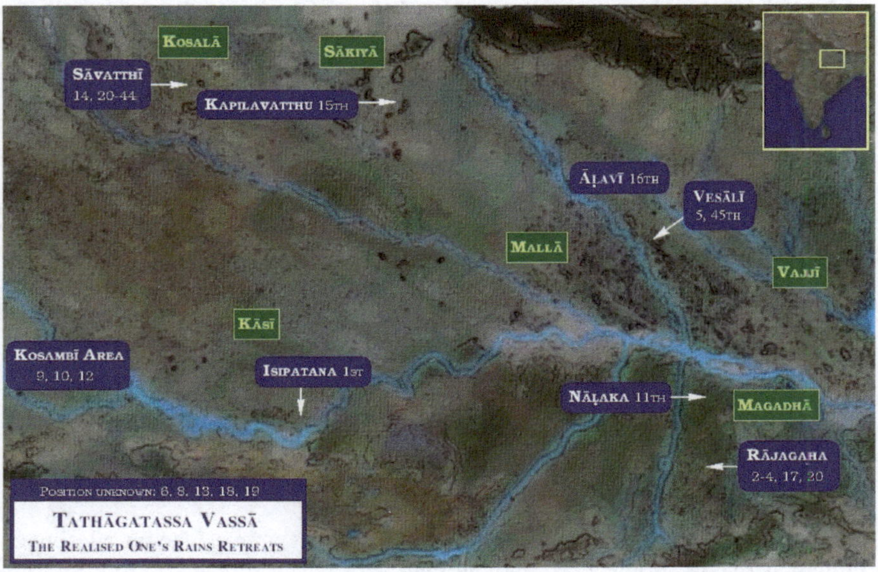

Fig. 3.3 Sites of the Buddha's Rains Retreats (*Note* Adapted from "The Realised One's rains retreats" by Ānandajoti Bhikkhu, 2012 [https://www.ancient-buddhist-texts.net/Maps/During-Buddhas-Time/Map-08-Vassa.htm]. Reprinted with permission [*Credit* Ānandajoti Bhikkhu])

The *Thapatisutta* (SN 55.6, SuttaCentral, 2020, paras. 1–16) records an example that is consistent with many found across the *Suttas* providing the place, the names and positions of the people involved, recording the cultural protocols that were followed, and the use of the familiar repetition to carry the consistency of the message through the text:

> *At Sāvatthī, at that time several mendicants were making a robe for the Buddha, thinking that when his robe was finished and the three months of the Rains residence had passed the Buddha would set out wandering. Now at that time the chamberlains Isidatta and Purāṇa were residing in Sādhuka on some business. They heard about this. So, they posted someone on the road, saying:*
>
> *"My good man, let us know when you see the Blessed One coming, the perfected one, the fully awakened Buddha." And that person stood there for two or three days before they saw the Buddha coming off in the distance. When they saw him, they went to the chamberlains and said:*
>
> *"Sirs, the Blessed One, the perfected one, the fully awakened Buddha is coming. Please come at your convenience."*
>
> *Then the chamberlains went up to the Buddha, bowed, and followed behind him. And then the Buddha left the road, went to the root of a tree, and sat down on the seat spread out. The chamberlains Isidatta and Purāṇa bowed, sat down to one side, and said to the Buddha:*
>
> *"Sir, when we hear that you will be setting out from Sāvatthī to wander in the Kosalan lands, we're sad and upset, thinking that you will be far from us. And when we hear that you will be setting out from the Kosalan lands to wander in the Mallian lands, we're sad and upset, thinking that you will be far from us."*
>
> *"And when we hear that you will be setting out from the Mallian lands to wander in the Vajjian lands … in the Kāsian lands …in the Māgadhan lands …."*
>
> *"But when we hear that you will be setting out from the Māgadhan lands to wander in the Kāsian lands, we're happy and joyful, thinking that you will be near to us. And when we hear that you are setting out from the Māgadhan lands to wander in the Kāsian lands … in the Vajjian lands … in the Mallian lands … in the Kosalan lands …to wander to Sāvatthī, we're happy and joyful, thinking that you will be near to us. And when we hear that you are staying near Sāvatthī in Jeta's Grove, Anāthapiṇḍika's monastery we have no little happiness and joy, thinking that you are near to us."*

Such examples, recorded across the *Suttas*, provide ample evidence that wandering, residing for short periods, teaching, and engaging in discussions with the people of each community was a familiar and repeated framing for the teaching work undertaken by the Buddha over the 45 years of his teaching in the heartland region.

3.2 Important Places of Teaching and Learning

There are four places that the Buddha recommended that people go to for pilgrimage: Lumbini, Uruvelā (Bodhgaya), Sarnath, and Kuśinagara. For the purposes of the focus of this book, I will highlight places of importance to teaching and learning. The first is Isipatana in the *Mrigadava* Deer Park where he gave his first teaching, the *Dhammacakkappavattanasutta* (SN 56.11, SuttaCentral, 2020) in which he taught the *cattari ariya saccani* Four Noble Truths and the *aṭṭhaṅgikaṃ maggaṃ* Noble

Eightfold Path (see Appendix C). The *Suttas* recount that seven weeks after his *nibbāna* enlightenment under a bodhi tree in Uruvelā (now known as Bodhgaya—see Fig. 3.2), the Buddha travelled to Isipatana to re-join his fellow seekers, with whom he had originally begun his journey to deepen his spiritual understanding. It was here he first formulated his educational philosophy, drawn from his direct experience and laid down his Middle Way approach (SN 56.11, SuttaCentral, 2020, paras. 1–2):

> *Thus, have I heard. On one occasion the Blessed One was dwelling at Bārāṇasī in the Deer Park at Isipatana. There the Blessed One addressed the bhikkhus of the group of five thus:*
>
> *"Bhikkhus, these two extremes should not be followed by one who has gone forth into homelessness. What two? The pursuit of sensual happiness in sensual pleasures, which is low, vulgar, the way of worldlings, ignoble, unbeneficial; and the pursuit of self-mortification, which is painful, ignoble, unbeneficial. Without veering towards either of these extremes, the Tathagata has awakened to the middle way, which gives rise to vision, which gives rise to knowledge, which leads to peace, to direct knowledge, to enlightenment, to Nibbāna."*

Another important place of teaching and learning was Rājagaha (now Rajgir), one of the emerging influential commercial towns at the centre of the kingdom of Māgadha. Here the teaching of the Buddha was endorsed by King Bimbisara, allowing the Buddha the freedom to return to this area many times in his teaching career. He spent time here for Rains Retreats in his early to mid-teaching career (see Fig. 3.3: According to Ānandajoti Bhikkhu, there are records for Years 2–4, 17 and 20) and the Buddha gave many important teachings in this area. Numerous *Suttas* begin with the Pāḷi phrase such as is found in the *Pāsāṇasutta* (see, e.g., SN 4.11, SuttaCentral, 2020, para. 1):

> *Ekaṃ samayaṃ bhagavā rājagahe viharati gijjhakūṭe pabbate ...*
>
> *On one occasion the Blessed One was dwelling at Rājagaha on Mount Vulture's Peak...*

The important site nearby to *Gijjhakūṭe* Mount Vulture's Peak was ancient Nalanda university, located in the vicinity of Rajgir. The contemporary Nalanda University was founded in 2010 at Rajgir rather than at the original heritage site. At the time of the Buddha, Nalanda was already an established place of higher learning that was basically a meeting place for discussions between teachers who held different views on the nature of the pathway to spiritual development, and in particular, inner wisdom, Brahmins, Jains and the Buddha and their respective followers. The Buddha often stayed near Nalanda, in Pāvārika's mango grove, giving teachings to individuals and groups and advice, drawn from the teachings he had been giving to kings and other tribes. As one example (SN 42.6, SuttaCentral, 2020, paras. 1–2):

> *At one time the Buddha was staying near Nālandā in Pāvārika's mango grove. Then Asibandhaka's son the chief went up to the Buddha, bowed, sat down to one side ...*

And again, in the *Vassakārasutta* (AN 7.22, SuttaCentral, 2020, paras. 1–3):

> *So, I have heard. At one time the Buddha was staying near Rājagaha, on the Vulture's Peak Mountain. Now at that time King Ajātasattu Vedehiputta of Māgadha wanted to invade the*

Vajjis. He declared: "I shall wipe out these Vajjis, so mighty and powerful! I shall destroy them, and lay ruin and devastation upon them!"

And then King Ajātasattu addressed Vassakāra the brahmin minister of Māgadha, "Please, brahmin, go to the Buddha, and in my name bow with your head to his feet. Ask him if he is healthy and well, nimble, strong, and living comfortably. And then say: 'Sir, King Ajātasattu Vedehiputta of Māgadha wants to invade the Vajjis. He says, "I shall wipe out these Vajjis, so mighty and powerful! I shall destroy them, and lay ruin and devastation upon them!"' Remember well how the Buddha answers and tell it to me. For Realized Ones say nothing that is not so."

In Chap. 2, I examined the influence of the Brahminical education system and the emergence of the Jains as another influential group of spiritual thinkers and educators. The Buddha would have been involved in conversations, debates, and public conferences hosted by kings. After the Buddha's passing, Nalanda went on to become a famous place of learning for Buddhists, as will be discussed later in this chapter. Davids (1911, pp. 102–103) makes the observation that such places were also well-located on old and new trade routes that navigated both the geographical features of the region and also its local politics that saw many wars, alignments, and re-alignments of the socio-economic order. Understandably, in this context, the Buddha would have sought protection from powerful kings, chiefs, and merchants and would have returned to places where he could dwell in safety, be fed and clothed, to sleep and bathe. These patrons enabled the Buddha to return many times to teach in these places and also undertook the important work of supporting his growing *Sangha* community of monks, at first and later also nuns, a group of people that can be credited with undertaking the impressive task of codifying his teachings, preserving them, and disseminating them across Asia, and latterly, to the world.

3.3 Dhamma Education in the Heartland

The EBTs depict an emerging urban life with flourishing trade, regional development and struggles between the various kingdoms as they began to form as towns and then cities. As discussed, the Buddha was teaching at a time of great uncertainty and upheaval. He was teaching in a time before the formation of the more rigidly understood caste system and the Buddha found support from traders who didn't fit with the old society, kings who were expanding their regional influence, and farmers who maintained some level of independence and time for spiritual development. Kings and local chiefs arranged for numbers of families to be responsible for feeding and clothing the Buddha and his followers, and they apportioned lands and built accommodations for them as their numbers grew. They also arranged for meeting halls to be converted from older buildings or built from new, but much of the Buddha's teaching was done in the open air, accessible to all who were interested, in common with other Indigenous traditions of teaching and learning. The Buddha's lessons were not secret and shared only to those students with inherited rights as was the case in the Brahminical education tradition; as will be discussed in greater detail in the following chapters, his was a curriculum of both secular and spiritual aspects, and he taught according to peoples' capacities to understand his ideas, supported by the knowledge they gained through the arising of their individual experiential understanding. His was a tailored curriculum with underlying core ideas gradually taught and developed as the learner matured in their understanding of their inner experiences.

Over 45 years, walking between the towns of what became known as the heartland of Buddhism, he connected deeply with the issues that were concerning to people. It is possible from reading the EBTs to gather a detailed picture of his life, his discussions, and his teachings, where he also engaged with them about questions and challenges that were being posed about his teachings by others, particularly as the numbers of his followers grew. A key aspect that I want to draw attention to in this section is that he was teaching using the traditional tools of an oral culture. Nothing was written down as yet. From the time of the Buddha's first speech Isipatana in the *Mrigadava* Deer Park in c.456 BCE until his passing in c.411 BCE, people were able to able to listen to the Buddha himself.

3.3.1 Orality, Rhetorics, and Memorisation

Over time, his *Sangha* of senior monks, nuns and laypeople began to memorise his teachings. In the first instance, this would likely have been to make sure to remember his approach and words in the months where he was away from their community visiting others. Without the benefit of a written text (Davids, 1899/2013; Gombrich, 2013; Sujato & Brahmali, 2015), people undertook to memorise the teachings of the Buddha while also preserving the elements of rhetoric and orality that demonstrate his pedagogy as well as organising its content Quintilian (95 CE/1921), in his beautiful 12 volume textbook on orality and rhetorics *Institutio Oratoria* (Institutes of Oratory, 1920) helpfully observed that:

> *The art of oratory, as taught by most authorities, and those the best, consists of five parts—invention, arrangement, expression, memory, and delivery or action (the two latter terms being used synonymously). But all speech expressive of purpose involves also a subject and words. If such expression is brief and contained within the limits of one sentence, it may demand nothing more, but longer speeches require much more. For not only what we say and how we say it is of importance, but also the circumstances under which we say it. It is here that the need of arrangement comes in. But it will be impossible to say everything demanded by the subject, putting each thing in its proper place, without the aid of memory. It is for this reason that memory forms the fourth department. But a delivery, which is rendered unbecoming either by voice or gesture, spoils everything and almost entirely destroys the effect of what is said. Delivery therefore must be assigned the fifth place.* (Book 3, Section 3, paras. 1–3)

I will employ Quintilian's five-part analysis to frame my analysis of the aspect of oratory employs by the Buddha to teach the *Buddha-Dhamma*. The first four parts—invention, arrangement, expression, and memory will be examined in this chapter. I will examine the fifth part, delivery, in Chaps. 4 and 5.

3.3.1.1 Invention

As discussed in Chaps. 1 and 2 (this edition), the Buddha was able to transform the tacit knowledge he learned from his teachers and his experiences into a format that was teachable. The Buddha's corpus of work, from his original utterances, were transformed using the techniques of arrangement, memorisation, and attention. This approach of the Buddha, also reflected in the observations made by Quintilian, and developed by oral societies over previous millennia, incorporated familiar elements of socialisation and education found in Indigenous and other traditionally-oriented societies. Goody (1968, 1977, 1986, 1987) and Ong (1982) argued for the importance of understanding orality and its relationship to the written word. I extended this observation (Ma Rhea, 2012) to argue that the use of orality, rhetorics, and memorisation continues to the present in many Indigenous and traditionally-oriented societies (see also, Langton & Ma Rhea, 2003; Living Knowledge Project, 2008; Marika-Mununggiritj & Christie, 1995; Marika, 1998; Yunupingu, 1994). I noted that students living in oral cultures have high levels of orality, memorisation, spatial, and rhetorical skills that teachers from literate cultures need to understand in order to create learning pathways to literacy development.

3.3.1.2 Arrangement

During the time of the Buddha, as mentioned, his *Sangha* of senior monks, nuns, and laypeople began to memorise his teachings. There are *Suttas* that record the Buddha telling his *Sangha* how to order his teachings to support his pedagogy of 'step by step' gradual learning, to be discussed in greater detail in Chap. 4. By way of example, in the *Gotamakacetiyasutta* (AN 3.125, SuttaCentral, 2020, paras. 1–3) it is recorded that:

> *On one occasion the Blessed One was staying near Vesālī at Gotamaka Shrine. There he addressed the monks, "Monks!"*
>
> *"Yes, lord," the monks responded.*
>
> *The Blessed One said, "It's through direct knowledge that I teach the Dhamma, not without direct knowledge. It's with a cause that I teach the Dhamma, not without a cause. It's with marvels that I teach the Dhamma, not without marvels. Because I teach the Dhamma through direct knowledge and not without direct knowledge, because I teach the Dhamma with a cause and not without a cause, because I teach the Dhamma with marvels and not without marvels, there is good reason for my instruction, good reason for my admonition. And that is enough for you to be content, enough for you to be gratified, enough for you to take joy that the Blessed One is rightly self-awakened, the Dhamma is well-taught by the Blessed One, and the community has practiced rightly".*

There are also Suttas that record him correcting two monks in their approach to teaching the Dhamma. In one example, in the *Ovādasutta* (SN 16.6, SuttaCentral, 2020, paras. 1–9), it is recorded that:

At Rājagaha in the Bamboo Grove. Then the Venerable Mahakassapa approached the Blessed One, paid homage to him, and sat down to one side. The Blessed One then said to him: "Exhort the bhikkhus, Kassapa, give them a Dhamma talk. Either I should exhort the bhikkhus, Kassapa, or you should. Either I should give them a Dhamma talk or you should."

"Venerable sir, the bhikkhus are difficult to admonish now, and they have qualities which make them difficult to admonish. They are impatient and do not accept instruction respectfully. Here, venerable sir, I saw a bhikkhu named Bhaṇḍa, a pupil of Ānanda, and a bhikkhu named Abhiñjika, a pupil of Anuruddha, competing with each other in regard to their learning, saying: 'Come, bhikkhu, who can speak more? Who can speak better? Who can speak longer?'"

Then the Blessed One addressed a certain bhikkhu thus: "Come, bhikkhu, tell the bhikkhu Bhaṇḍa and the bhikkhu Abhiñjika in my name that the Teacher calls them."

"Yes, venerable sir," that bhikkhu replied, and he went to those bhikkhus and told them: "The Teacher calls the venerable ones."

"Yes, friend," those bhikkhus replied, and they approached the Blessed One, paid homage to him, and sat down to one side. The Blessed One then said to them: "Is it true, bhikkhus, that you have been competing with each other in regard to your learning, as to who can speak more, who can speak better, who can speak longer?"

"Yes, venerable sir."

"Have you ever known me to teach the Dhamma thus: 'Come, bhikkhus, compete with each other in regard to your learning, and see who can speak more, who can speak better, who can speak longer'?"

"No, venerable sir."

"Then if you have never known me to teach the Dhamma thus, what do you senseless men know and see that, having gone forth in such a well-expounded Dhamma and Discipline, you compete with each other in regard to your learning, as to who can speak more, who can speak better, who can speak longer?"

This method of discussion and correction among the *Sangha* and laypeople continued during the lifetime of the Buddha, and scholars of the EBTs accept that these recordings, available as they are now to us in books and digital formats provide the most reliable body of work by which to assess the authenticity of them (Gombrich, 2013). As such, the arrangement of the oral teachings continued after the passing of the Buddha (c. 411 BCE). Hecker (1987) provides a detailed account of the role of Maha Kassapa in leading to the eventual preservation of what became known as the *Tipitaka*. Of relevance to this monograph, soon after the Buddha's funeral observances had been made, Maha Kassapa suggested to King Ajātasattu of Magadha that, in order to protect the teachings, that a conference should be called of 500 monks, to gather at the caves of *Gijjhakūṭe* Mount Vulture's Peak near Rājagaha to deliberate on the arrangement of the teachings. It was at this meeting, extending over many months, that along with other key elements, Ananda began the process of laying down the discourses with questioning and clarifications from the other monks. Ananda was recognised as having a uniquely accurate memory of the Buddha's teachings, and here the 5 *Nikāya* collections of the *Sutta Pitaka* were arranged and codified for the first time at what has come to be known as the First Buddhist Council. The monks continued the work begun by the Buddha, living the same lifestyle, bound by the same rules, and teaching as far as was possible, an accurate version of the teachings. Important too was the injunction by the Buddha that the *Sangha* of monks and nuns should teach according to their direct experience. There was no 'leader' of the growing Buddhist *Sangha* and their *sekhas* learners. From about 300 BCE, one hundred years later, with the advent of writing, there was a development from a tradition of oral teaching to writing down the teachings of the Buddha of these trusted disciples of the First Council. The Second and Third Buddhist Councils maintained the commitment to recitation of the *Sutta Pitaka* orally, and the Fourth Council held in Sri Lanka in about 83 B.C., during the reign of the pious Sinhalese king, Vatta Gamani Abhaya, a Council of Arahants was held in Sri Lanka and the *Tipitaka*, for the first time in the history of Buddhism, was put down in writing on ola leaves. Writing became necessary because in a time of great hardship and famine, the *dhammabhāṇakas* dhamma reciters and monks were dying of starvation and there was concern that the teachings would be forgotten. The Mahavamsa (2007, para. 26) *r*ecords that:

> *The text of the three pitakas and the atthakatha thereon did the most wise bhikkhus hand down in former times orally, but since they saw that the people were falling away (from religion) the bhikkhus came together, and in order that the true doctrine might endure, they wrote them down in books.*

3.3.1.3 Memorisation

After the passing of the Buddha, monks and nuns became the teachers of the Buddha's system of education. There were *Sangha* and lay teachers using both the Buddha's techniques for teaching and his core teachings. This work was supported by the same kings, wealthy merchants, and clan chiefs as had been during the Buddha's time and many of these individuals erected monasteries for the *Sangha*, arranged for them to be fed and clothed by appointed villagers, such was the value perceived by these benefactors for themselves and for the people they were responsible for protecting. Having secured a place for the Sangha within the turbulent, emerging society in transition occurring around them, the *Sangha* now had safe places in which to live and begin the significant task, historically speaking, of codifying the body of knowledge that was the legacy from the Buddha. We can surmise much of what occurred after this early period before the *Tipitaka* was written down through the *Suttas* where the Buddha encouraged the *Sangha* to begin these processes of arranging, discussing, rearranging the body of work and the behaviours associated with teaching it, evaluating its usefulness to the people who were learning it, and continuing to teach as the Buddha had done. Within this work, the role of memorisation is a key pedagogical device that is maintained by the *Sangha* to the present day. The *Sangha* followed the conventions of oratory and rhetorics that would have been familiar to Quintilian and to the many teachers in Indigenous societies whose responsibility was to pass on cultural and spiritual knowledge to future generations (Sato & Diamond, 2020).

As Gombrich (2013, p. 8) observes of the *Suttas*, and the importance of memorisation, '… many texts do purport to reproduce the Buddha's sermons. If in doing so they employ various of the conventions of oral literature, schematising the material by the use of formulae and stock passages, this is no argument against their essential authenticity'. While scholars such as Sujato and Brahmali (2015) and Gombrich (2013) are concerned to establish the legitimacy of the *Suttas*, in this monograph, I have concurred with their approach and have taken the EBTs to be a reliable record. In doing so, it becomes possible to analyse them for the oratorical conventions that the *Sangha* used. I will go into more detail of these techniques in Chaps. 4 and 5 (this edition), because they are the cornerstones of the Buddha's pedagogical approach. In this example, in the *Adhammavagga* the Buddha gives straightforward instruction of the importance of differentiating what was good teaching and not good teaching (AN 1.142–149, SuttaCentral, 2020, para. 3), repeating the same form with slight variation to emphasise each aspect, expounding that:

> *"Those mendicants who explain what … was not spoken and stated by the Realized One as not spoken and stated by the Realized One … what was spoken and stated by the Realized One as spoken and stated by the Realized One … what was not practiced by the Realized One as not practiced by the Realized One … what was practiced by the Realized One as practiced by the Realized One … what was not prescribed by the Realized One as not prescribed by the Realized One … what was prescribed by the Realized One as prescribed by the Realized One … are acting for the welfare and happiness of the people, for the benefit, welfare, and happiness of gods and humans. They make much merit and make the true teaching continue."*

Here I will recount an example of a layperson named Khujjuttarā. According to the Pāḷi commentaries, she was a maid to the Queen of Kosambi, and she memorised the teachings of the Buddha while in the service of the Queen during his teachings. Bhikkhu Bodhi's footnote suggests that she was a servant of Sāmāvatī, another of the Buddha's lay followers and that Khujjuttarā would 'go to hear the Buddha's teachings and then repeat his discourses for the ladies of the court' (Bhikkhu Bodhi, 2012, p. 1610, ff. 141). The Buddha remarked that 'The foremost of my laywomen … who are very learned is Khujjuttarā' (AN 1.258–267, SuttaCentral, 2020, paras. 1–3). Her feats of memorisation were recorded in the *Itivuttaka*, a collection of 112 short discourses in mixed prose and verse found in the *Khuddakanikāya Minor Collection*, described as being arranged in the Aṅguttara style of ascending numbered sets, from one to four (Ireland, 1997; *Itivuttaka*, SuttaCentral, 2020).

Her story reminds us that it was the work of many people over countless generations that have used memorisation to preserve these teachings, some recognised in the *Tipitaka* for their willingness and abilities, but many more whose commitments to the preservation and dissemination of the Buddha's teachings has been done by millions of *dhammabhāṇakas* dhamma reciters, *dhammadutas* messengers of the dhamma, and all other teachers, for individuals, communities, regions, nations, and continents over these last 100 generations. The delivery aspect of oratory, the fifth aspect noted by Quintilian, will be examined in Chap. 4. The next section moves to a description of how the Buddha's system of education was disseminated beyond the Buddhist heartland across Asia and then to the world.

3.3.2 Disseminating the Dhamma in the First Wave

While still relying on the oral conventions of arrangement, memorisation and delivery, the *Sangha* of *bhikkhus* monks and *bhikkhunis* nuns spread out from the heartland, continuing the practices established by the Buddha. Like its modern counterparts, most of these teachers would have taught in the languages of their birth and in Pāḷi, other Prakrits, and Sanskrit if they were able. Over time, there were some who undertook the significant work of translation into local dialects as people beyond the heartland heard of the teachings and wanted the *Sangha* to travel to their kingdom, republic, or region to pass on these teachings.

The Second Buddhist Council that met at Vesālī, in Bihar province, about 100 years after the First Council, appears to have added little to the codification work. There was a dispute about rules for the *Sangha* but no record of disagreements about the EBTs. This suggests that teachers continued to attract people who were interested in the Buddha's teachings during this period. This first phase of development was the establishment of Buddhist monasteries across India through 400–300 BCE enabling the *Sangha* of *bhikkhus* monks and *bhikkhunis* nuns to travel further in all directions, probably doing as the Buddha had done, moving between villages and towns over the year as the seasons and the needs of kings, chiefs, merchants, and farming communities required.

The Third Buddhist Council was a different affair and marked a concerted change in the way that Buddhism became spread across Asia. Under the patronage of King Aśoka (c. 268–232 BCE), he hosted the third Buddhist Council in Pataliputra (near present-day Patna, Bihar Province), after many months of deliberation, disputes between different teachers and sects were examined and debated under the leadership of the monk Moggaliputta Tissa. This was an important and very public examination of the monks who were present. The king asked suspect monks what the Buddha taught, and they claimed he taught views that did not exist in the *Tipitaka.* The king then asked virtuous monks about the same issues, and they replied that with answers that were confirmed by Moggaliputta Tissa. The Council recited the full 5 *Nikāya.* The orthodox teachings of the Buddha were reaffirmed so that the original teachings remained.

The other significant development at this time was that of writing. This was to have a profound effect on the world but also contributed to the spread of Buddhism. King Aśoka became known for his Edicts, phrases of the *Dhamma* carved into stone pillars in the Brahmi script (Salomon, 1998, p. 17), a modern term used to refer to the left-to-right 'Indo-Pāḷi' script of the Aśokan pillar inscriptions. He used these written inscriptions to remind people to live a good life. Over time, in places such as Nalanda and other monasteries, the task of writing down the oral teachings was slowly beginning, but it is clear that by the time of King Aśoka that there were people who were able to read these inscriptions.

On the wave of possibilities realised by the Third Council with its royal patronage, the leader of the Third Council, Moggaliputta Tissa organised and dispatched evangelical missions to distant lands. For instance, Majjhantika went to Kashmir and Gandhara, Majjhima led the party to the Himalaya country, Mahadeva was deputed to Mahisamandala (Mysore), Sona and Uttara to Suvarnabhumi (Burma), Mahadharmaraksita and Maharaksita were sent to Maharastra and the Yavana country respectively, and Ashoka's son Mahendra, who had become a monk, was sent along with others to Sri Lanka (Ceylon). This Third Council encouraged the spread of Buddhism into both Sri Lanka and also to Burma and Thailand following the oral tradition of exposition, undertaken by monks and nuns who had been trained in the oral tradition. This Southeast Asian version of Buddhism has become known as Theravādan Buddhism, the smaller vehicle. It would not be until the Fourth Buddhist Council held at the Anuradhapura Maha Viharaya in Sri Lanka that the *Tipitaka* would be fully committed to the written form.

3.4 Disseminating the Dhamma in the Second Wave

Monks were also sent out from Nalanda University to spread Buddhism across the regions to the West, North, and Northeast of the Buddhist heartland. The teachings became known as those of the Mahayana schools, the larger vehicle that was designed to be shared with laypeople. Some doctrinal difference began to develop at places of early learning such as Nalanda, and as Buddhist ideas were disseminated out from Nalanda by missionary monks and translated into local communities with their tribal languages, gods and spirits, Buddhism began its processes of absorption into all the places and communities on its journeys (Fig. 3.4).

3.4.1 Nalanda: From Monastery to Disseminator of Buddhism Across Asia

The highly formalised methods study of the *Tipitaka* developed by the Buddha, and codified by the *Sangha*, and subsequent Buddhist Councils helped the establishment of large teaching institutions such Nalanda. Prior to the Buddha, as discussed in Chap. 2, the centres of Brahmanical education were the *āśrama* hermitages where students lived in close personal touch with their preceptor. It was a select group who were eligible for this sort of higher training. Banerjee (1977, pp. 2–3) observes that:

> *With the advent of Buddhism, the picture completely changed. Buddhism came as a challenge to the Brahminical orthodoxy and insularism in the field of religion and the teachings of the Buddha gave a complete reorientation to the educational system that was in vogue those days.*

Nalanda found royal patronage at various times as archaeological and epigraphic materials show and at its peak the school attracted scholars and students from the region from places such as China, where news of this centre of learning about Buddhism had spread. After a fairly settled period of regional expansion in the Buddhist heartland, Buddhist ideas began to spread along the trade routes spanning

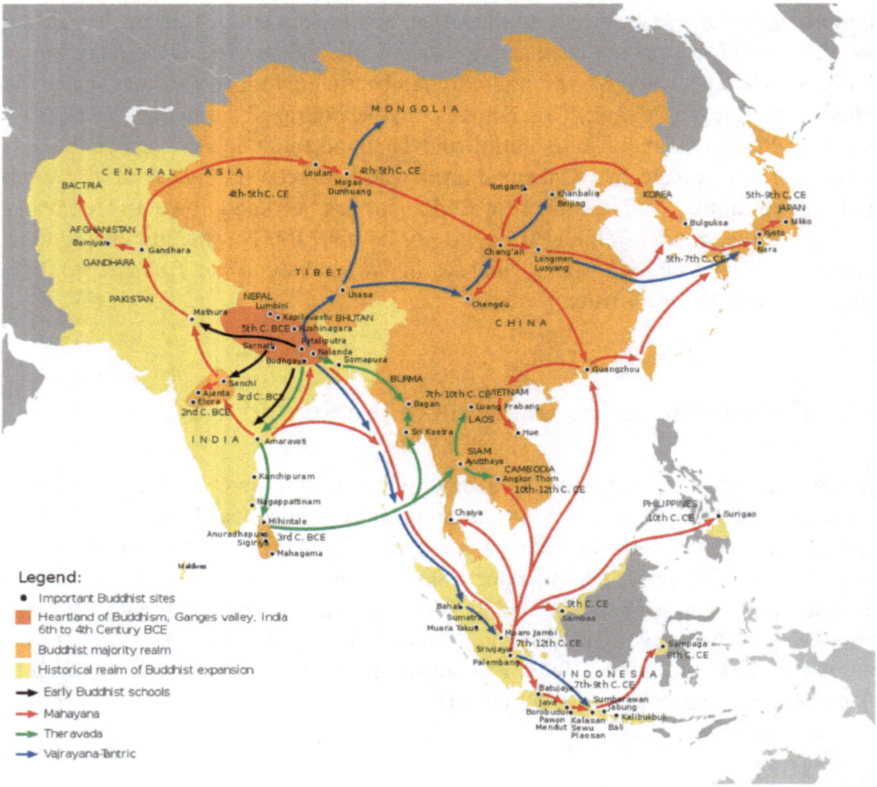

Fig. 3.4 The spread of Buddhism (*Note* Adapted from "Buddhist Expansion" by Gunawan Kartapranata (his work combined and redrawn from various sources), 2014. [https://commons.wikimedia.org/w/index.php?curid=30905152]. CC License)

from China into western Asia and beyond. Faxian is known to have undertaken travels to India in about 399 AD when he was 60 years old. Bhikku Ānandajoti (2013, paras. 7–9) notes that:

> … detailed information about Faxian is hard to come by and precise dates and locations are difficult to pin down. He ordained as a child in China, and seems to have become more and more discontent with the lack of authentic texts in the country, especially those pertaining to the Discipline (Vinaya). He set out from China to go to the West in 399 around the age of 60 and spent maybe ten years or more years there, before traveling to Sri Lanka where he spent a further two years. During the sea route from Sri Lanka back to China he stopped off somewhere in either Sumatra or Java. After returning he spent the rest of his life recording his travels, especially concerning the practices he found in India, and translating the texts he had brought back, and died at the ripe old age of eighty-eight.

More detailed records are available about the pilgrimage of Xuanzang (Hiuen-tsiang).

Banerjee (1977, p. 13) credits: 'To Hiuen-tsiang and I-tsing we are indebted for a vivid description of academic life at Nalanda University'. Xuanzang (also spelt as

Hiuen-tsiang) spent a number of years at Nalanda. His records provide fascinating account of the journey taken by him from China, his place of birth, in search of clarification of the Buddha's teachings that he felt had become distorted over time. He says:

> *...only distant people coming to interpret the doctrine (the sounds of his doctrine, emphasis in original) are not in agreement. The time of the Holy One is remote from us: and so, the sense of his doctrine is differently expounded. But as the taste of the fruit of different trees of the same kind is the same so the principles of the schools as they now exist are not different. The contentions of the North and South have indeed many hundreds of years agitated our land with doubt, and no able master has been found able to dispel them.* (Hwui-li & Beal, 1911, pp. 31–32)

The records begin with information about his birth (Hwui-li & Beal, 1911) and of his journey from China to Nalanda University and back over a period of 17 years. He recorded that he left China in 630 AD (Hwui-li & Beal, 1911, p. 11) returning after learning all he had sought to learn at Nalanda and other places of learning in the heartland of Buddhism and along the roads that he travelled (Fig. 3.5).
Xuanzang records that the lands of the Nalanda area were gifted to the Buddha by 500 merchants who purchased it for him so that he could teach them the Dhamma (Hwui-li & Beal, 1911, p. 110). He also provides confirmation of many of the teachings and teaching approaches used by the Buddha during his life (see Chaps. 4 and 5,

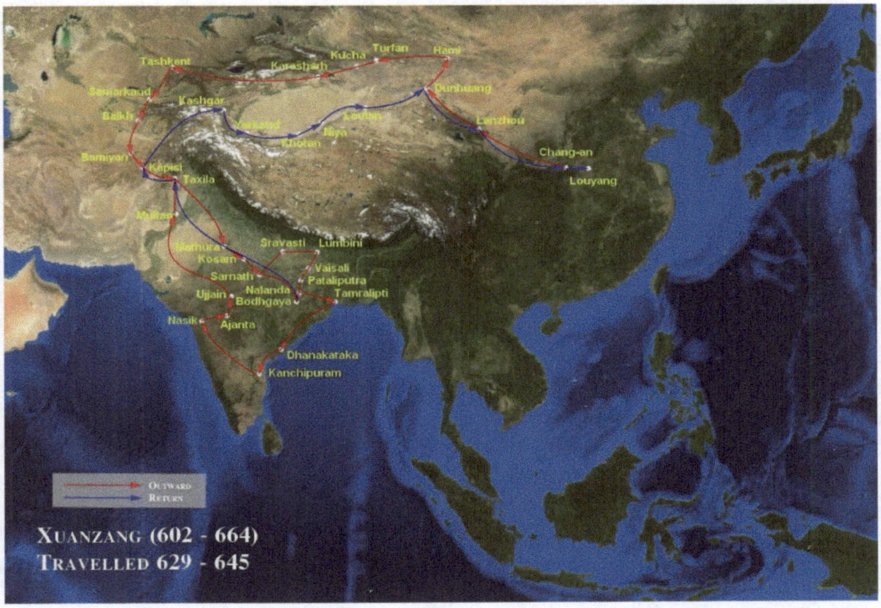

Fig. 3.5 The pilgrimage of Xuanzang (*Note* Adapted from "Chinese Pilgrims to Central Asia, India and SE Asia: Xuanzang, 600-664" by Ānandajoti Bhikkhu, 2012 [https://www.ancient-buddhist-texts.net/Maps/Silk-Routes/Chinese-Pilgrims.htm]. Reprinted with permission [*Credit* Ānandajoti Bhikkhu])

this edition) and as they were preserved by the *Sangha* at the First Buddhist Council (Hwui-li & Beal, 1911, pp. 115–117; Xuanzang, 1906, pp. 162–164). He was received at Nalanda after three years of travel and describes details of his life there. He records that: 'Within the temple they arrange every day about 100 pulpits for preaching, and the students attend these discourses without fail even for an inch shadow on the dial' (Xuanzang, 1906, p. 109). Banerjee (1977, p. 14); (Gold, 2008) provides a succinct summary of Xuanzang's records of the curriculum studied by students:

> *...the five vidyās, the five-fold traditional subjects of study in those days, viz., (i) Śabdavidyā (Grammar and Philosophy), (ii) Cikitsāvidyā (Medicine), (iii) Hetuvidyā (Logic), (iv) Śilpasthānavidyā (Fine Arts) and (v) Adhyātmavidyā (Metaphysics).*

Xuanzang also provides commentary that the curriculum included teachings from the Great Vehicle (*Mahāyāna*), the works belonging to the 18 (*Hīnayāna*[2]) Sects, the Vedas (Banerjee, 1977, p. 14). Xuanzang completed the aim of his pilgrimage saying:

> *He thoroughly investigated the language (words and phrases), and by talking with those men on the subject of the 'pure writings' he advanced excellently in his knowledge. Thus, he penetrated, and examined completely, all the collection (of Buddhist books) and also studies the sacred books of the Brahmans during 5 years.* (Hwui-li & Beal, 1911, p. 125)

Xuanzang returned to China by the southern route continuing to teach and discuss the Buddha's teachings as he travelled. He returned finally to China and settled to undertake the significant translation work that would allow his new knowledge to be disseminated across the region in order to correct some of the disputes that had developed over the centuries.

Archaeological remains found along the old southern Silk Road, and the more northern Tea Horse Road provide evidence for the spread of *Mahāyāna* Buddhism from 400 to 500 CE. By 600 CE, these ideas had spread from the Korean peninsula into Japan, creating *Zen* Buddhism and south to Indonesia in 700 CE. In 800 CE, a particular version of Buddhism known as *Vajrayana* travelled from Nalanda north to Lhasa, Tibet and then onto Dunhuang and onto Mongolia. Dunhuang, being on the crossroads of the Silk Road and this norther route holds invaluable objects and history of the spread of Buddhism still being discovered.

Important from an education point of view, this history remains consistent with the Buddha's pedagogy to teach people in their mother tongue, an approach that continues to be subject of debate in cross-cultural education to the present day. Each time the Buddha's teachings reached a new tribe with a new language, the painstaking work of translation began. Wooden block, carved in reverse would be made by monks and then printed into the local language. Much of this work has been destroyed, but there remain some precious examples held in museums around the world.

---

[2]This term is no longer used to describe what is also collectively known as Theravāda Buddhism because the Sanskrit meaning of *Hīnayāna* suggest that this form of Buddhism is deficit to the 'better' Greater Vehicle teachings. The term Nikaya Buddhism, suggested by Nagatomi is also used for the early schools. Both newer terms, Theravāda and Nikaya will be used in preference to describe the 18 Sects unless quoting original sources.

3.4.2 Consolidation of Dhamma Education Principles in the Historical Realms

This period of Asian expansion certainly saw a proliferation of explanations and ideas about Buddhism and its teachings that grew in the fertile soil of each location that lasted has endured. I examined the Buddhist influences on the modern education system in Thailand (Ma Rhea, 2013, 2017) noting that historically in Thailand where the practices of Theravāda Buddhism were adopted, formal studies were conducted in the *wat* temple by monks who were also senior, revered members of the local community. Only boys were allowed to attend the *wat* temple for formal studies, as was the case during the early period of the Buddha's time, and consistent with the Brahminical education tradition. Formal studies comprised learning the ways of knowing in the three domains of *sila* morality, *samadhi* concentrations, and *vipassana* insight understanding. The *wat* temple was, by definition, a place for cultivating *paññа* 'higher' wisdom. Still in Buddhist countries such as Thailand, people predominantly are encouraged to learn by experience, using local knowledge for both daily and spiritual activities. In time the *wat* temple expanded to teach a more secular curriculum, creating the possibility of an approach to knowledge that was not embedded in the Buddhist world view. The *wat* temples also began to teach girls. The oldest *Maha Chulalongkorn Ratchawitthayalai* University (MCU) still draws from traditional Thai Buddhism for its principles of operation with Faculties of Buddhist Studies, Education, Humanities, Social Sciences, a Graduate School, and an International Buddhist Studies College. Together with *Maha Makutta Ratcha Witthayalai*, both Buddhist universities were made public universities in 1997.

Other publicly-funded universities were established to pass on outsider knowledge, such as development knowledge, that was derived from European education systems. This was incorporated into Thai universities as university knowledge. This outsider secular knowledge became a distinct hallmark of universities to distinguish them from the Buddhist education system but importantly, these universities also strive through their extracurricular activities and overall ethos to complement Thai ways of thinking deeply influenced by the teachings and pedagogical approach first developed by the Buddha. Thai people described their local knowledge as being derived from the even older *phumpanjaachawbaan* rural wisdom, significantly shaped by Thai Buddhism, and being passed on through Thai socialisation strategies that were geared to giving young members of the society the knowledge they needed in order for them to be able to be 'Thai'. These ways of thinking, knowing and doing things were either formally taught by older family or community members or informally acquired by the young through observation. These processes of formal and informal acquisition of local knowledge continued throughout a person's life; the shape of the knowledge changed over time and was context-based, and the storehouses were available to all in the community.

This pattern can be seen repeated across Asia, that as the teachings and the pedagogies of the Buddha were spread by missionary monks as *Nikaya* Early Buddhism both south in the first wave and north, west, and east in the second, we see a process

I have named 'adaptive balancing' (Ma Rhea, 1997a, 1997b, 2000) that took ancient education practices for life, both mundane and spiritual, grounded them in predominantly rural, Indigenous, and traditionally-oriented kingdoms, free republics, and the emerging commercial towns and engaged people in taking the teachings, practising them, gaining direct experience from the methods that would, in turn, be developed into ways of living that over time have become influenced by Buddhism but might look different in the present era. As Banerjee (1977) reminds us, the taste is the same even if the fruit has grown from different trees of the same type.

3.5 Global dissemination of the Dhamma in the third wave

Notably, the first contact between the West and Buddhism occurred when Alexander the Great of Greece conquered India between 300 and 125 BCE during the first wave of expansion. Some of the Greek colonists who remained in India became Greco-Buddhists, and their contribution to Buddhism in philosophy and iconography is still recognised. From settlements in Bactria, they contributed some of the early artistic representations of the Buddha in places such as Gandhara and inscriptions on coins during the rule of Menander 1.

The next phase of expansion to Western nations occurred many years later in what I am determining to be the third wave. The scattering of the Tibetan people foreseen by Padmasambhava has certainly come to pass as has the new wave of expansion of the Buddhist teachings across the planet. For example, Buddhism is one of the fastest-growing religions in Australia with the Australian Bureau of Statistics (2017, para. 4) noting that, 'Australia is increasingly a story of religious diversity, with Hinduism, Sikhism, Islam, and Buddhism all increasingly common religious beliefs'.

In 2020, Buddhists were estimated to make up 7% of the global population (Pew Research Centre, 2015), in 2020 estimated to be about 10%. Buddhism does not seem to be growing in Asia but is doing so through its adoption by people of other religions across the world. While it is complicated to assess the impact of switching, the stories of migration of Asian Buddhist to a country such as Australia, together with those born in Australia showing signs of switching from former Christian affiliation or being unaffiliated is being revealed through migration, and national census data sees a history of Buddhism beginning to emerge in such countries. The same is being revealed in the UK, France, Germany, the United States, Canada, and New Zealand. Concurrently, there is also a growing interest in the ideas of Buddhism and their inclusion in education thinking. Croucher (1989), for example, traced the history of Buddhism in Australia from 1848 to 1988 and found that while there are Buddhist communities in Australia that have migrated from Southeast Asia, there are also significant numbers of Australians who travelled to Asia and brought Buddhism back, at least in some of its philosophical and Dhamma forms if not culturally.

In this time of the 'iron eagle flying', an eighth-century prophecy attributed to Padmasambhava (see also, Bhikkhuni Ayya Khema, 1991), it seems to be quite amazing that the core teachings have remained the same during this past 2,500 years.

The pedagogical pathway to the cultivation of wisdom can still be found in common curriculum elements across Theravada, Mahayana, and Vajrayana traditions that include: The same Vinaya, the Five Precepts, and have as their foundation the Four Noble Truths. The *aṭṭhaṅgikaṃ maggaṃ* Noble Eightfold Path is the guiding curriculum, and there is the use of scriptures of the *Tipitaka* Buddhist Canon: the three baskets (*Vinaya Pitaka, Sutta Pitaka,* and *Abhidhamma Pitaka*) albeit with some variations according to tradition (see Appendix A and B). Equally, when Buddhism comes to places like Australia or England or America, it doesn't then come into contact with an Indigenous people with locally developed lifeways, with their distinctive histories, languages, and educational approaches as was the case during the first and second wave of dissemination of Buddhism that occurred from 2,500 years ago until about 1,200 years ago.

After a period of stabilisation across Asia, this new third wave has occurred differently because of colonisation and migration (Smith, 2003). Colonisation by European powers across Asia and places like Australia is now, itself, being influenced by a recursive loop where Buddhism is being introduced to those nations and their former colonies through migration and travel. I see an emerging mix of a European tribal sort of indigeneity, if you like, mixing with the philosophical ideas of the Buddha. The research by Smith (2003, p. 9) is showing that there is an interesting interplay between indigeneity and colonisation. She describes this interplay with sharp evocation:

> *On the northern shores of Australia there are two stands of banyan trees, a legacy of the early Buddhists in Australia which serves as a reminder of the past for future generations. Sinhalese cane cutters who had arrived in Mackay to angry racist protests and hard labour in the cane fields during the 1870-80 s found solace and a compatriot community with pearlers on Thursday Island. There, as an expression of spiritual identity and as a gift for perpetuity, they planted two bodhi trees (Ficus religiosa) from cuttings that had been imported from a venerated tree in Ceylon (now Sri Lanka). In the heart of Darwin stands another banyan, known in the local language as Galamarrma (Ficus virens), which has been an old friend to generations of Indigenous Larrakia people and a place to meet, trade, post notices and ponder for generations still. To the immigrant Chinese in the latter half of the nineteenth century, the tree was a familiar beacon that provided sanctity in an alien and often brutal landscape. This banyan became known as the Tree of Knowledge, in no small part because, as the accompanying plaque reads: It was also a place where Chinese youth met with, and learned from, their elders and where wisdom was gained in its shade. In the new land, Confucian, Tao and Buddhist traditions combined and have continued.*

This meeting of philosophies and cultures is more sharply defined in a multicultural nation such as Australia where Buddhism is now navigating its relationship with Australia's Aboriginal and Torres Strait Islander peoples, is being practised by immigrant Buddhist communities from Asia, and is also being taken up by non-Indigenous settler Australians whose ancestors are from other places and predominantly Christian. In the realm of education, it is being learnt about informally through temples and other Buddhist organisations and also brought into formal mainstream education systems through the establishment of schools and universities that are guided by the Buddha's educational philosophy.

In 2002, an edited collection of foundational interest to this monograph (Hori et al., 2002) contained many important insights into a newly emerging research field. Focused predominantly on the teaching of the Buddha's core curriculum in Western universities. Few then were focusing on the pedagogical aspects of the Buddha's teaching. Foundational in their insights, chapters by Wotypka (2002) and Jarow (2002) are two of few to grapple with pedagogical elements, a matter I will examine in greater detail in Chaps. 4 and 5 (this edition). In 2012, the International Association of Buddhist Universities hosted a conference at *Maha Chulalongkorn Ratchawitthayalai* University (MCU) on the theme 'Teaching Dhamma in New Lands' where scholars of Buddhism reported on their research in a wide variety of countries about myriad aspects facing teachers of the Dhamma, whether *Sangha* or lay teachers, in both formal and informal settings (see, e.g., Marpet, 2012; Mon, 2012; Thero Kannadeniye, 2012; Ven Chu, 2012). Underscoring this variety was the enduring reference point of the teachings of the Buddha preserved in the EBTs and of his pedagogical approach. In 2013, among an extensive collection of research notes encompassing an encyclopedia of 'Sciences and Religions' (Runehov & Oviedo, 2013) is a note by Borup (2013) that provides insight into the story of Buddhism's spread to the West and its engagement with Western science. Research scholarship about Buddhist Studies has blossomed in the ensuing year. A remarkable aspect of these edited collections, and subsequent emerging scholarship, is that this field stands as a testament to the enduring and dynamic nature of Buddhism and its ability to adapt to the learning preferences of many different peoples from many different cultures. It is to this remarkable adaptability that I now turn, in the next chapter to more thoroughly examine the Buddha's pedagogical approach and its enduring characteristics.

References

Suttas

SuttaCentral. (2020). Aṅguttara Nikāya 4.183. *Sutasutta* On What is Heard. [Bhikkhu Thanissaro, Trans.]. Retrieved December 31, 2020 from https://suttacentral.net/an4.183/en/thanissaro. Translated from the Pāḷi by Thanissaro Bhikkhu. The text of this page is licensed under a Creative Commons Attribution—Non Commercial 4.0 International License. To view a copy of the license, visit http://creativecommons.org/licenses/by-nc/4.0/. Documents linked from this page may be subject to other restrictions. Transcribed from a file provided by the translator. Access to Insight (Legacy Edition), 30 November 2013, http://www.accesstoinsight.org/. Prepared for SuttaCentral by Gabriel Laera and Ayya Vimala.

SuttaCentral. (2020). Aṅguttara Nikāya 4.53. *Paṭhamasaṃvāsasutta* Living Together. [Bhikkhu Bodhi, Trans.]. Retrieved December 31, 2020 from https://suttacentral.net/an4.53/en/bodhi. The Numerical Discourses of the Buddha (Wisdom Publications, 2012). This excerpt from The Numerical Discourses of the Buddha by Bhikkhu Bodhi is licensed under a Creative Commons Attribution—Non Commercial - No Derivs 3.0 Unported License. Based on the work The Numerical Discourses of the Buddha at Wisdom Publications. Permissions beyond the scope of this license may be available at Wisdom Publications. Prepared for SuttaCentral by Blake Walsh.

SuttaCentral. (2020). Aṅguttara Nikāya 7.22. *Vassakārasutta* With Vassakāra. [Bhikkhu Sujato, Trans.]. Retrieved December 31, 2020 from https://suttacentral.net/an7.22/en/sujato. Translated for SuttaCentral by Bhikkhu Sujato, 2018. Dedicated to the public domain via Creative Commons Zero (CC0). You are encouraged to copy, reproduce, adapt, alter, or otherwise make use of this translation in any way you wish. Attribution is appreciated but not legally required.

SuttaCentral. (2020). *Itivuttaka*. [J. D. Ireland, Trans.]. Retrieved December 31, 2020 from https://suttacentral.net/iti. Translated from the Pāḷi by John D. Ireland. Digital Transcription Source: BPS Transcription Project. Extracted from The Udāna & the Itivuttaka, translated and introduced by John D. Ireland. Published in 1997. The complete book, including introduction and notes by the translator, is available from the Buddhist Publication Society. ISBN 955–31-0164-X. This text has been made available by the kind permission of the Buddhist Publication Society. It was released under the following licence terms: For free distribution. This work may be republished, reformatted, reprinted and redis-tributed in any medium. However, any such republication and redistribution is to be made available to the public on a free and unrestricted basis, and translations and other derivative works are to be clearly marked as such. Prepared for SuttaCentral by Bhikkhu Sujato.

SuttaCentral. (2020). *Saṃyuktāgama* 236. The meditative abode of emptiness-concentration. [Trans C. Mun-keat, Trans.]. Retrived December 15 2020 from https://suttacentral.net/sa236/en/choong. The meditative abode of emptiness-concentration. Translation by Choong Mun-keat (Wei-keat), 2004. Originally published in Choong Mun-keat (Wei-keat), The Notion of Emptiness in Early Buddhism, 1995, 1999. Used by permission of the translator. Prepared for SuttaCentral by Bhikkhu Sujato.

SuttaCentral. (2020). Saṃyutta Nikāya 4.11. *Pāsāṇasutta* The Boulder. [Bhikkhu Bodhi, Trans.]. Retrieved December 31, 2020 from https://suttacentral.net/sn4.11/en/bodhi. The Connected Discourses of the Buddha (Wisdom Publications, 2000). This excerpt from The Connected Discourses of the Buddha by Bhikkhu Bodhi is licensed under a Creative Commons Attribution—Non Commercial—No Derivs 3.0 Unported License. Based on the work Connected Discourses of the Buddha at Wisdom Publications. Permissions beyond the scope of this license may be available at Wisdom Publications. Prepared for SuttaCentral by Blake Walsh.

SuttaCentral. (2020). Aṅguttara Nikāya 1.142–149. *Adhammavagga*. Not the teaching. [Trans. Bhikkhu Sujato, Trans.]. Retrieved December 30, 2020 from https://suttacentral.net/an1.140-149/en/sujato. Translated for SuttaCentral by Bhikkhu Sujato, 2018. Dedicated to the public domain via Creative Commons Zero (CC0). You are encouraged to copy, reproduce, adapt, alter, or otherwise make use of this translation in any way you wish. Attribution is appreciated but not legally required.

SuttaCentral. (2020). Aṅguttara Nikāya 1.258–267. *Sattamavagga*. Seventh. [Trans. Bhikkhu Sujato, Trans.]. Retrieved December 30, 2020 from https://suttacentral.net/an1.258-267/en/sujato. Translated for SuttaCentral by Bhikkhu Sujato, 2018. Dedicated to the public domain via Creative Commons Zero (CC0). You are encouraged to copy, reproduce, adapt, alter, or otherwise make use of this translation in any way you wish. Attribution is appreciated but not legally required.

SuttaCentral. (2020). Aṅguttara Nikāya 3.125. *Gotamakacetiyasutta* At Gotamaka Shrine. [Trans. Bhikkhu Thanissaro, Trans.]. Retrieved December 31, 2020 from https://suttacentral.net/an3.125/en/thanissaro. Translated from the Pāḷi by Thanissaro Bhikkhu. The text of this page is licensed under a Creative Commons Attribution—Non Commercial 4.0 International License. To view a copy of the license, visit http://creativecommons.org/licenses/by-nc/4.0/. Documents linked from this page may be subject to other restrictions. Transcribed from a file provided by the translator. Access to Insight (Legacy Edition), 30 November 2013, http://www.accesstoinsight.org/. Prepared for SuttaCentral by Gabriel Laera and Ayya Vimala.

SuttaCentral. (2020). Aṅguttara Nikāya 5.220. *Madhurāsutta* About Madhurā. [Trans. Bhikkhu Sujato, Trans.]. Retrieved December 31, 2020 from https://suttacentral.net/an5.220/en/sujato. Translated for SuttaCentral by Bhikkhu Sujato, 2018. Dedicated to the public domain via Creative

Commons Zero (CC0). You are encouraged to copy, reproduce, adapt, alter, or otherwise make use of this translation in any way you wish. Attribution is appreciated but not legally required.

SuttaCentral. (2020). Saṃyutta Nikāya 16.6. *Ovādasutta* Exhortation. [Trans. Bhikkhu Bodhi, Trans.]. Retrieved December 31, 2020 from https://suttacentral.net/sn16.6/en/bodhi. This excerpt from The Connected Discourses of the Buddha by Bhikkhu Bodhi is licensed under a Creative Commons Attribution—Non Commercial—No Derivs 3.0 Un-ported License. Based on the work Connected Discourses of the Buddha at Wisdom Publications. Permissions beyond the scope of this license may be available at Wisdom Publications. Prepared for SuttaCentral by Blake Walsh.

SuttaCentral. (2020). Saṃyutta Aṅguttara Nikāya 42.6. *Asibandhakaputtasutta.* With Asibandhaka's Son. [Trans. Bhikkhu Sujato, Trans.]. Retrieved December 31, 2020 from https://suttacentral.net/sn42.6/en/sujato. Translated for SuttaCentral by Bhikkhu Sujato, 2018. Dedicated to the public domain via Creative Commons Zero (CC0). You are encouraged to copy, reproduce, adapt, alter, or otherwise make use of this translation in any way you wish. Attribution is appreciated but not legally required.

SuttaCentral. (2020). Saṃyutta Aṅguttara Nikāya 55.6. *Thapatisutta* The Chamberlains. [Trans. Bhikkhu Sujato, Trans.]. Retrieved December 31, 2020 from https://suttacentral.net/sn55.6/en/sujato. Translated for SuttaCentral by Bhikkhu Sujato, 2018. Dedicated to the public domain via Creative Commons Zero (CC0). You are encouraged to copy, reproduce, adapt, alter, or otherwise make use of this translation in any way you wish. Attribution is appreciated but not legally required.

SuttaCentral. (2020). Saṃyutta Aṅguttara Nikāya 565.11. *Dhammacakkappavattanasutta* Setting in Motion the Wheel of the Dhamma. [Trans. Bhikkhu Bodhi, Trans.]. Retrieved December 15, 2020 from https://suttacentral.net/sn56.11/en/bodhi. Translated for SuttaCentral by Bhikkhu Bodhi, 2018. The Connected Discourses of the Buddha (Wisdom Publications, 2000). This excerpt from The Connected Discourses of the Buddha by Bhikkhu Bodhi is licensed under a Creative Commons Attribution—Non Commercial—No Derivs 3.0 Un-ported License. Based on the work Connected Discourses of the Buddha at Wisdom Publications. Permissions beyond the scope of this license may be available at Wisdom Publications. Prepared for SuttaCentral by Blake Walsh.

Authored Texts

Australian Bureau of Statistics. (2017). *2016 Census: Religion.* Retrieved December 15, 2020 from Australian Bureau of Statistics. https://www.abs.gov.au/AUSSTATS/abs@.nsf/mediareleasesbyReleaseDate/7E65A144540551D7CA258148000E2B85.

Banerjee, D. K. (1977). The ancient University of Nalanda. In C. S. Upasak (Ed.), *Nalanda past and present* (pp. 1–25). Nava Nalanda Mahavihara.

Bhante Ānandajoti. (2012). *Maps of Ancient Buddhist Asia.* Retrieved December 15, 2020 from Ancient Buddhist Texts. https://www.ancient-buddhist-texts.net/Maps/During-Buddhas-Time/Map-02-Early-Career.htm.

Bhikkhu Bodhi. (2012). *The numerical discourses of the Buddha.* Wisdom Publications.

Bhikkhuṇi Ayya Khema. (1991). *When the iron eagle flies: Buddhism for the West.* Penguin Books.

Bhikku Ānandajoti. (2013). *Chinese pilgrims to Central Asia, India and SE Asia.* Retrieved December 17, 2020 from Ancient Buddhists Texts. https://www.ancient-buddhist-texts.net/Maps/Silk-Routes/Chinese-Pilgrims.htm.

Borup, J. (2013). Buddhism in the West. In A. L. C. Runehov & L. Oviedo (Eds.), *Encyclopedia of sciences and religions.* Dordrecht: Springer. https://doi.org/10.1007/978-1-4020-8265-8_157.

Croucher, P. (1989). *Buddhism in Australia, 1848–1988.* New South Wales University Press.

Davids, T. W. R. (1899/2013). *Dialogues of the Buddha* (Vol. 1). Pāḷi Text Society.

Davids, T. W. R. (1911). *Buddhist India.* Kessinger Publishing.

Gold, J. C. (2008). *The dharma's gatekeepers: Sakya Pandita on Buddhist scholarship in Tibet*. SUNY Press.

Gombrich, R. F. (2013). *What the Buddha thought*. Equinox Publishing Ltd.

Goody, J. (Ed.). (1968). *Literacy in traditional societies*. Cambridge University Press.

Goody, J. (1977). *The domestication of the savage mind*. Cambridge University Press.

Goody, J. (1986). *The logic of writing and the organisation of society*. Cambridge: Cambridge University Press.

Goody, J. (1987). *The interface between the written and the oral*. Cambridge University Press.

Hecker, H. (1987). *Maha Kassapa: Father of the Sangha* (Nyanaponika Thera, Trans.; Vol. 345). Wheel Publications.

Hori, V. S., Hayes, R. P., & Shields, J. M. (Eds.). (2002). *Teaching Buddhism in the West: From the wheel to the web*. RoutledgeCurzon.

Hwui-li, S., & Beal, S. (1911). *The life of Hiuen-Tsiang*. Kegan Paul, Trench, Trubner & Co. Reprinted by Facsimile Publisher, India for Gyan Books.

Ireland, J. D. (1997). *The Udāna & the Itivuttaka*. Buddhist Publication Society.

Jarow, E. H. R. (2002). The peripatetic class: Buddhist traditions and myths of pedagogy. In V. S. Hori, R. P. Hayes, & J. M. Shields (Eds.), *Teaching Buddhism in the West: From the wheel to the web* (pp. 107–118). RoutledgeCurzon.

Krishnan, G. P. (2008). *On the Nalanda trail: Buddhism in India, China, and Southeast Asia*. Asian Civilisations Museum.

Langton, M., & Ma Rhea, Z. (2003). *Traditional lifestyle and biodiversity use regional report: Australia, Asia and the Middle East. Composite report on the status and trends regarding the knowledge, innovations and practices of Indigenous and local communities*. United Nations Environment Programme. https://www.cbd.int/doc/meetings/tk/wg8j-03/information/wg8j-03-inf-04-en.doc.

Living Knowledge Project. (2008). *About 'both ways' education*. Retrieved December 15, 2020 from Living Knowledge. http://livingknowledge.anu.edu.au/html/educators/07_bothways.htm.

Ma Rhea, Z. (1997a). Gift, commodity and mutual benefit: Analysing the transfer of university knowledge between Thailand and Australia. *Higher Education Policy: The Quarterly Journal of the International Association of Universities, 10*(2), 111–120. https://www.academia.edu/729015/Gift_commodity_and_mutual_benefit_analysing_the_transfer_of_university_knowledge_between_Thailand_and_Australia.

Ma Rhea, Z. (1997b). University knowledge exchange: Gift, commodity and mutual benefit. *Californian Sociologist, 17*(18), 211–250.

Ma Rhea, Z. (2000). Contemporary knowledge production and reproduction in Thai universities: Processes of adaptive balancing. In G. R. Teasdale & Z. Ma Rhea (Eds.), *Local knowledge and wisdom in higher education* (pp. 209–235). Pergamon Elsevier.

Ma Rhea, Z. (2012). Thinking Galtha, teaching literacy: From Aboriginal mother tongue to strangers' texts and beyond. In A. Cree (Ed.), *Aboriginal education: New pathways for teaching and learning* (pp. 31–53). Australian Combined University Press.

Ma Rhea, Z. (2013). Buddhist wisdom and modernisation: Finding the balance in globalized Thailand. *Globalizations, 10*(4), 635–650. https://doi.org/10.1080/14747731.2013.806739.

Ma Rhea, Z. (2017). *Wisdom, knowledge, and the postmodern University in Thailand*. Palgrave Macmillan. https://doi.org/10.1057/978-1-137-37694-7.

Marika-Mununggiritj, R., & Christie, M. J. (1995). Yolngu metaphors for learning. *International Journal of the Sociology of Language, 1995*(113), 59–62. https://doi.org/10.1515/ijsl.1995.113.59.

Marika, R. (1998). The 1998 Wentworth lecture. *Australian Aboriginal Studies, 1*, 3–9. https://search.informit.com.au/documentSummary;dn=128495525811423;res=IELAPA.

Marpet, B. (2012). *The Beatnik Buddhist: The Monk of American Pop-Culture* Teaching Dhamma in New Lands, Ayutthaya, Thailand. https://www.scribd.com/doc/95848066/IABU-2012-Teaching-Dhamma-in-New-Lands.

Mon, S. Y. (2012). *Exporting Dharma to New Lands: Empirical approaches of teaching dharma in predominantly non-Buddhist states*. Teaching Dhamma in New Lands, Ayyuthaya, Thailand. https://www.scribd.com/doc/95848066/IABU-2012-Teaching-Dhamma-in-New-Lands.

Muecke, S. (2011). Australian Indigenous philosophy. *CLCWeb: Comparative Literature and Culture, 13*(2), Article 3. https://doi.org/10.7771/1481-4374.1741.

Nonaka, I., & Takeuchi, H. (1995). *The knowledge creating company: How Japanese companies create the dynamics of innovation*. Oxford University Press.

Ong, W. J. (1982). *Orality and literacy: The technologizing of the word* (2nd ed.). Routledge.

Parsaye, K., & Chignell, M. (1988). *Expert systems for experts*. Wiley.

Pew Research Centre. (2015). *The future of world religions: Population growth projections, 2010–2050*. https://assets.pewresearch.org/wp-content/uploads/sites/11/2015/03/PF_15.04.02_ProjectionsFullReport.pdf.

Polanyi, M. (1958,1998). *Personal knowledge: Towards a post critical philosophy*. Routledge.

Quintilian. (95 CE/1921). *The Institutio Oratoria of Quintilian* (H. E. Butler, Trans.; T. E. Page, E. Capps, W. H. D. Rouse, L. A. Post, & E. H. Warmington, Eds. Vol. III). William Heinemann (Original work published 95 CE).

Runehov, A. L. C., & Oviedo, L. (Eds.). (2013). *Encyclopedia of sciences and religions*. Dordrecht: Springer. https://doi.org/10.1007/978-1-4020-8265-8.

Salomon, R. (1998). *Indian epigraphy: A guide to the study of inscriptions in Sanskrit, Prakrit, and the other Indo-Aryan languages*. Oxford University Press.

Sato, C., & Diamond, Z. M. (2020). An Indigenous history of education in Japan and Australia. In P. J. Anderson, K. Maeda, Z. M. Diamond, & C. Sato (Eds.), *Post-imperial perspectives on Indigenous education: Lessons from Japan and Australia* (pp. 25–65). Routledge. https://doi.org/10.4331/9780429400834-3.

Smith, M. K. (2003). *Michael Polanyi and tacit knowledge*. The encyclopedia of pedagogy and informal education. Retrieved November 11, 2010 from infed.org: education, community-building and change. https://infed.org/mobi/michael-polanyi-and-tacit-knowledge/.

Sujato, & Brahmali, Bhikkhu. (2015). *The authenticity of the early buddhist texts*. Chroniker Press. https://ocbs.org/wp-content/uploads/2015/09/authenticity.pdf.

The Mahavamsa. (2007). *The ten kings*. The Mahavamsa.org Retrieved December 17, 2020 from The Mahavamsa. http://mahavamsa.org/mahavamsa/original-version/33-ten-kings/.

Thero Kannadeniye, S. (2012). *Challenges Sri Lankan monks face in Disseminating Dhamma to children in the US*. Teaching Dhamma in New Lands, Ayutthaya, Thailand. https://www.scribd.com/doc/95848066/IABU-2012-Teaching-Dhamma-in-New-Lands.

Ven Chu, C. (2012). *Teaching dharma in the United States*. Teaching Dharma in New Lands, Ayutthaya, Thailand. https://www.scribd.com/doc/95848066/IABU-2012-Teaching-Dhamma-in-New-Lands.

Wotypka, J. (2002). Engaging Buddhism: Creative tasks and student participation. In V. S. Hori, R. P. Hayes, & J. M. Shields (Eds.), *Teaching Buddhism in the West: From the wheel to the web* (pp. 95–106). RoutledgeCurzon.

Xuanzang. (1906). *Si-Yu-Ki: Buddhist records of the Western world* (S. Beal, Trans.). Kegan Paul, Trench, Trubner & Co. Reprinted by Gacsimile Publishers, India for Gyan Books.

Yunupingu, M. (1994). Yothu Yindi—Finding balance. *Race and Class, 35*(4), 113–120. https://doi.org/10.1177/030639689403500412.

Zeng, B. (2017). Research progress in Indigenous ecological knowledge in natural resource management. *Journal of Australian Indigenous Issues, 20*(2), 69–86. https://search.informit.com.au/documentSummary;dn=149417815145958;res=IELIND.

Chapter 4
Buddha's *Pavīṇaupāya* 'by Skilful Means' Pedagogy

Abstract This chapter makes the transition from an emphasis on the broader historical and sociocultural aspects that influenced the educational approach taken by the Buddha towards an examination of the Buddha as an adult educator with a clear pedagogical intent. This chapter will make a close examination of the various pedagogical approaches used by the Buddha that supported his teaching of the *Buddha-Dhamma* core curriculum of the *cattari ariya saccani* Four Noble Truths and the *aṭṭhaṅgikaṃ maggaṃ* Noble Eightfold Path. These approaches include some that would be familiar to the modern reader, some that have fallen out of favour, or some more akin to Indigenous and traditionally-oriented approaches to pedagogy that continue to be employed by teachers.

Keywords Buddhist pedagogy · *Buddha-Dhamma* core curriculum · *cattari ariya saccani* Four Noble Truths · *aṭṭhaṅgikaṃ maggaṃ* Noble Eightfold Path · *Pavīṇaupāya* 'by skilful means' pedagogy

4.1 Introduction with a Note on Methods of Analysis

Previous chapters have laid the groundwork for a detailed examination of the Buddha as a teacher. The first chapter set the scene for the development of the Buddha's teachings and his teaching approach, linking his educational methods to the historical context in India 2,500 years ago. I briefly introduced what we know of how the people of that time thought about teaching and learning.

The second chapter provided a more in-depth examination of the Buddha's 45-year education legacy. Examining what is known about teaching and learning at that time, the chapter chartered the emergence of the Buddha's education theory introduced through an overview of the *cattari ariya saccani* Four Noble Truths and the *aṭṭhaṅgikaṃ maggaṃ* Noble Eightfold Path from the *Tipitaka* Buddhist Canon, the as the *Buddha-Dhamma* 'core curriculum'. This *Buddha-Dhamma* core curriculum and the *Majjhima Patipada* Middle Way approach to teaching provide an outline of the broad canvas of his educational theory.

In Chap. 3, I presented historical evidence about aspects of education in the region in northern India where the Buddha spent his teaching life, known as the heartland

Z. M. Diamond, *Gautama Buddha*, https://doi.org/10.1007/978-981-16-1765-2_4

of Buddhism, and explored the process of generation, codification, and preservation of the *Tipitaka* Buddhist Canon and its dissemination after the passing of the Buddha from its heartland in India. I then examined the second wave of adaptations across the Asian region, the consolidation over about 800 years until the more recent third period of adaptation globally with Buddhist acclimatisation in the West through informal teaching and learning contexts.

This chapter makes a transition from an emphasis on broader historical and socio-cultural aspects on the educational approach taken by the Buddha (Chaps. 1–3, this edition) towards an examination of the Buddha as a teacher, turning to an analysis of his key teaching and learning approaches that have been preserved and transmitted orally and in writing for over 2,500 years. Through examining the key elements of his *Majjhimā Paṭipadā* Middle Way approach found in the *Tipitaka* Buddhist Canon, this chapter will elucidate the pedagogical approach employed by Gautama Buddha in his teaching (Fig. 4.1).

First discussing the Buddha as a teacher, the chapter then considers the ideal qualities and characteristics of the teacher, disciple and learner in the Buddha's approach. The final sections focus on the pedagogical approach taken by the Buddha to the task of teaching and learning: drawn from content analysis of the relevant early Buddhist *suttas*, the pedagogical techniques used by the Buddha to deepen learning will be described. These pedagogical devices are found most commonly in an array of traditionally-oriented societies where orality was a key element of teaching and learning. The chapter will tease out the importance of these pedagogical devices for modern education, in particular the experiential element.

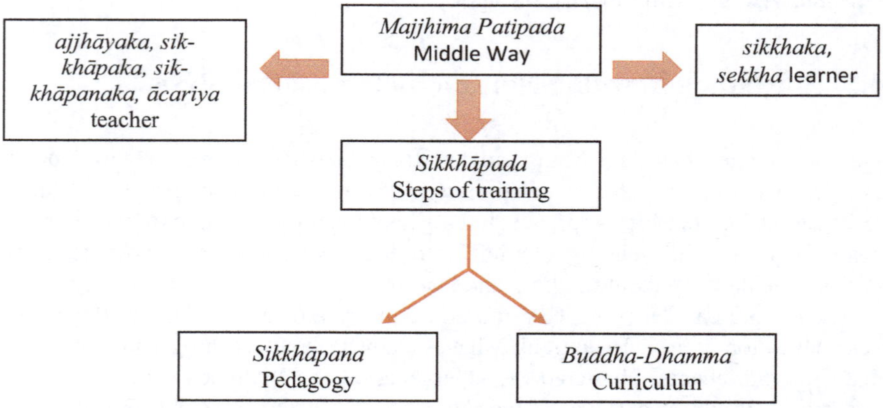

Fig. 4.1 Overview of the Buddha's education approach

4.1.1 Methods

For this chapter, I have undertaken a content analysis of the EBTs using the technique of qualitative content analysis as described by Mayring (2000). Content analysis enables systematic text analysis. In this case, I drew on the considerable digital work being undertaken by Buddhists on the web-based repository called SuttaCentral (https://suttacentral.net/). *SuttaCentral* contains a significant, and growing, repository of all known EBTs in as many languages as have been possible to transfer into digital form (SuttaCentral, 2020). Having access to the EBTs in digital form has allowed me to search across digital texts in a manner that was impossible before this resource became available. In doing so, I was able to demonstrate evidence of the considerable attention that the Buddha gave to discussing his approach to teaching as much he discussed his educational philosophy and core teachings. The keywords I focused on for the content analysis were the and English and Pāḷi word for:

- teach *uggaṇhāpeti* (Buddhadatta Mahathera, 1958, p. 52)
- teacher *ajjhāyaka* (Buddhadatta Mahathera, 1958, p. 4); *sikkhāpaka*, *sikkhāpanaka* (Buddhadatta Mahathera, 1958, p. 281); *ācariya* (Buddhadatta Mahathera, 1958, p. 40)
- teaching, instruction and training *ajjhāpana* (Buddhadatta Mahathera, 1958, p. 4); *sikkhāpana* (Buddhadatta Mahathera, 1958, p. 281);
- learn *uggaṇhāna*; *uggaṇhāti*; *uggaṇhiya* (Buddhadatta Mahathera, 1958, p. 52); *sikkhāti* (with the meaning to 'train oneself, to practice') (Buddhadatta Mahathera, 1958, p. 281)
- learner *sikkhaka*; *sekkha* (Buddhadatta Mahathera, 1958, p. 302)
- learning and training *sikkhana* (Buddhadatta Mahathera, 1958, p. 281)

I searched each of the five *Sutta Nikāyas*, the *Dīghanikāya* (abbr. DN) Long Discourses containing 34 long suttas, the *Majjhimanikāya* (abbr. MN) Middle Discourses containing 152 medium-length suttas, the *Saṃyuttanikāya* (abbr. SN) Connected Discourses containing 7,762, shorter *Suttas*, the *Anguttaranikāya* (abbr. AN) Numbered Discourses, arranged numerically containing 9,565 short *Suttas* grouped by numbers from ones to elevens, and the *Khuddakanikāya* (abbr. KN) Minor Discourses, a mix of important teachings attributed to the Buddha and his disciples. I also referred to the hard copy EBTs from the Pāḷi Text Society (2020) and the online library of Buddhist texts and commentaries of the Buddhist Publication Society (2020) for cross-referencing and clarifications.[1]

[1]Following the convention as explained by Bhikkhu Bodhi, references to the *Dīghanikāya* (DN) Long Discourses and the *Majjhimanikāya* (MN) Middle Discourses refer to the number of the sutta. References to the *Saṃyuttanikāya* (SN) refer to the number of the chapter followed by the number of the sutta within that chapter. References to the *Anguttaranikāya* (AN) refer to *nipata* (numerical division) followed by the number of the sutta within that nipata (Bodhi, 1980, pp. 7–8).

I transferred records to word documents, pdfs, and csv files and then transposed each instance in an Excel spreadsheet. I then undertook a numerical count and developed emerging themes. From these raw records, I was able to undertake analysis across a range of similar examples to develop an understanding of the patterns that emerged from the initial analysis. These data were then collated into charts and tables for comparative purposes. My analysis was informed by Gombrich's (2012, p. 8) reminder that:

> *... the kind of analysis which can dissect a written philosophical tradition is inappropriate for oral materials. As I have shown, the texts preserving "the Buddha's word" are not authored in the same sense as a written text. While it is perfectly possible that some of the texts were composed by the Buddha himself, we cannot know this with any certainty, and almost all the texts are, strictly speaking, anonymous compositions.*

Even so, as Gombrich (2012) and Sujato and Brahmali (2015) also observe, the repetition techniques used by the preservers of the Buddha's teachings and approach across the EBTs point to a remarkable coherence of key concepts. This coherence is certainly revealed in the content analysis undertaken for this monograph.

4.2 Buddha's Ideas About Teaching and Learning: Key Findings

Description of the Buddha's pedagogical approach and educational philosophy is found across the Suttas. Those specifically about the key terms for teaching appear as follows (Table 4.1).

Notably, each of the *Sutta Nikāyas* expresses aspects of the Buddha's education philosophy and pedagogy with slightly different emphasis. The *Dīghanikāya* (DN) Long Discourses are presented as the Buddha being in dialogue with his followers and other interested people, with a strong emphasis on the relationship between the Buddha's teachings and other contemporary philosophies. Using repetition, he explains his core teaching (DN 10 and 15), his general approach to spiritual teaching and its development (DN 12), the ways in which his ideas and approach are compatible with other teachings (DN 25) and his method of teaching (DN 33).

Table 4.1 Teach, Teacher, Instruction, and Training word counts (English only; cross-checked with Pāli)

Sutta Nikāya collection	References
Dīghanikāya Long Discourses	740
Majjhimanikāya Middle Discourses	1,284
Saṃyuttanikāya Connected Discourses	1,421
Anguttaranikāya Numbered Discourses	154
Khuddakanikāya Minor Discourses (focus on the *Dhammapada*)	51

The *Majjhimanikāya* (MN) Middle Discourses provides many examples of how to teach his core curriculum. For example, his method for stopping unwanted thoughts (MN 20, SuttaCentral, 2020). Within the *Majjhimanikāya,* he demonstrates his use of figurative language (Simile of the Snake MN 22, Elephant's Footprint MN 27). He provides an overall template for organising his core teachings in the longer Simile of the Elephant's Footprint (MN 28, SuttaCentral, 2020). He deals with the intricacies of how to teach the concept of *paṭiccasamuppāda* dependent origination (MN 38, SuttaCentral, 2020). Bhikkhu Bodhi (1980) notes that the details of the content of this important teaching are found in other *Suttas* such as the *Saṃyuttanikāya,* the *Upanisasutta* (SN 12.23, SuttaCentral, 2020), teaching on Proximate Causes and the *Paṭiccasamuppādasutta* (SN 12.1, SuttaCentral, 2020), and the teaching on Dependent Origination. We find in the *Majjhimanikāya* that there is more focus on explanations given by the Buddha about how to teach his ideas. In MN 47, he gives an example of how to investigate his teachings and emphasises that different ways of teaching are appropriate for different contexts and should not be cause for dispute (MN 59). He encourages his students/learners/followers to seek experiential proof through their own examination of his teachings using methods he explains in detail (MN 80). In MN 118 and MN 119, he gives examples of how to investigate, for example, mindfulness of breathing and mindfulness of the body, practices that, through direct experience (as discussed in MN100) allow his students to develop their deeper understanding of his teachings. In this way, he teaches his students how to learn (MN 124).

The *Saṃyuttanikāya* provides numerous examples of the Buddha's teaching methods for general and more specific aspects of his core teachings. For example, the general exposition of his core teachings is given in SN 56, the *Sacca Saṃyutta* Linked Discourses on the Truths. This exposition contains 131 discourses on the four noble truths: suffering, its origin, its cessation, and the path (see Appendix C). These formed the main subject of the Buddha's first discourse, the *Dhammacakkappavattana Vagga* (SN 56.11, SuttaCentral, 2020). Of foundational importance to the topic of focus for this monograph, it is in this set of teachings that distinguishes the Buddha as a *samma sambuddha* one who could teach what he had discovered by his personal, direct experience. This particular aspect of being able to teach distinguished him from those known as *pacceka buddha* who might have had direct experiences but are not able to communicate their learnings in a teachable form (Bhikkhu Thanissaro, 2010).

In addition to such generally applicable overarching teachings, he also provides myriad examples of his pedagogical approach having key characteristic of using what would be known now as differentiated teaching and learning. These aspects are further discussed and developed in the following sections and in Chap. 5. Regarding particular aspects of teaching, he specifically explains the qualities of a teacher (SN 8.5) and gives a longer discussion on the characteristics of a teacher (MN 12.82–92). In his discussion with his son, Rāhula, he gives a step by step exposition of his method for his son to follow (SN 18.2–22, SuttaCentral, 2020). In a series of 12 discourses illustrating diverse points of the teachings (*Opammavagga* (SN 20.1–12, SuttaCentral, 2020)), his use of vivid simile is again highlighted as a key pedagogical technique. In the *Pālileyyasutta* (SN 22.81, SuttaCentral, 2020), the Buddha teaches in detail the 37 practices that lead to spiritual development and awakening. Here there is a clear pedagogical overview of his approach, consistent with other *Suttas*, his method is described, and he speaks here also of the need for the teacher to be able to assess what the student's question is and answer it in a way that can be understood (SN 22.81, SuttaCentral, 2020, paras 7–8):

> *Then the Venerable Ānanda together with those bhikkhus approached the Blessed One at Parileyyaka, at the foot of the auspicious sal tree. Having approached, they paid homage to the Blessed One and sat down to one side. The Blessed One then instructed, exhorted, inspired, and gladdened those bhikkhus with a Dhamma talk. Now on that occasion a reflection arose in the mind of a certain bhikkhu thus: "How should one know, how should one see, for the immediate destruction of the taints to occur?"*
>
> *The Blessed One, having known with his own mind the reflection in that bhikkhu's mind, addressed the bhikkhus thus ...*

In the *Okkantasaṁyutta* (SN 25.1–10, SuttaCentral, 2020), and in the *Pañcakaṅgasutta, Bhikkhusutta*, and *Sīvakasutta* (SN 36.19–21, SuttaCentral, 2020), the Buddha makes clear that he uses different techniques and examples because contexts are different. His teachings provide a similar point repeated for different student needs. For example, in a set of 10 teachings (SN 25.1–10, SuttaCentral, 2020), his emphasis is on different methods to be used for those who approach the teachings with faith and intellect or those who arrive by direct, personal experience. More broadly, there are many examples of the Buddha's use of the technique of differentiating the content to suit his student's needs. He taught differently to those who he assessed as being ready or not, used examples that would be of meaning to the individual kings, Brahmins, monks, laity, merchants, farmers, women and men, young and old, and always towards the end of a teaching he circled around to checking with that person for their understanding.

In the *Saṃyuttanikāya* there is also repeated use of numbers to order and organise the teachings, an aspect that is consistent with the pedagogical needs of oral transmission of information and something that becomes less necessary in a written form. The Suttas in general are replete with lists of numbered teachings. For example, the *Indriya Saṃyutta* (SN 48) known as the Linked Discourses on the Faculties contains 178 discourses on various sets of *indriya* faculties. The teachings repeat, in various forms, the five key *indriya* of faith, energy, mindfulness, immersion, and wisdom expanding to discourses on a wider range of 22 faculties, including the six sense faculties, five kinds of feeling, three faculties relating the process of attaining *nibbāna* enlightenment, and three concerning biology and gender. It is noted in the explanation for the *Indriya Saṃyutta* (SN 48, SuttaCentral, 2020)[2] that 'this flexible category thus serves as a link between the teachings on wisdom and those on the path'.

This aspect is exemplified in the *Anguttaranikāya* where teachings about numbers of things are grouped together as the ones, the twos etc. It provides a different approach to the same content and is an invaluable tool for finding examples of

[2]See expanded description under the *Indriya Saṃyutta* tab (https://suttacentral.net/sn48).

an appropriate length and complexity for the capacity of the student or audience. This collection also contains evidence of another key characteristic of the Buddha's pedagogical approach, that it is a gradual teaching approach. In the *Aṭṭhakanipāta* Book of Eights, in the *Pahārādasutta* (AN 8.19, SuttaCentral, 2020) the first stanza encapsulates his approach. He first asks a question framed to have eight aspects, thereby supporting the memory of the eight (para. 17):

> *"The bhikkhus see eight astounding and amazing qualities in this Dhamma and discipline because of which they take delight in it. What eight?"*

He then explains his pedagogical approach to the teaching of the first of the eight qualities of the *Buddha-Dhamma* as being gradual, similar to a great ocean (AN 8.19, SuttaCentral, 2020, para. 18), saying that:

> *"Just as, Pahārāda, the great ocean slants, slopes, and inclines gradually, not dropping off abruptly, so too, in this Dhamma and discipline penetration to final knowledge occurs by gradual training, gradual activity, and gradual practice, not abruptly. This is the first astounding and amazing quality that the bhikkhus see in this Dhamma and discipline because of which they take delight in it."*

This approach of gradual teaching is also echoed, for example, in MN 65, 70, and 107. This pattern is repeated in the *Anguttaranikāya* where teachings scattered across the other collections are gathered and formalised according to the number of key aspects contained therein. Similarly, the *Khuddakanikāya* Minor Discourses contains, is a wide-ranging collection of fifteen books containing complete *suttas*, verses, and smaller fragments of *Dhamma* teachings. This collection preserves much of the Buddha's teachings in formats that were recorded, reproduced, and remembered over centuries. They are not 'minor' teachings in the sense of their importance because there are many valuable collections contained within the *Khuddakanikāya* that serve as curriculum. The famous one is the *Dhammapada* (Dhp, SuttaCentral, 2020), path of the Dhamma, but there are also many other. The *Dhammapada* alone contains 51 references to teaching and eight to learning, giving a succinct introduction to the core curriculum (see Appendix C, this edition).

Overall, the five books of the *Sutta Nikāya* provide ample evidence of the coherence of the Buddha's education philosophy, overall pedagogical approach to teaching and learning (next section). These *Nikāyas* also provide myriad examples of pedagogical techniques that support gradual and differentiated learning. The next section gives some examples of the qualities and characteristics of the Buddha as a teacher and of teachers more generally.

4.3 The Buddha as a Teacher

The first aspect to note is that, at first, when the Buddha had followed his personal path to developing his inner wisdom to its conclusion, he was reluctant to turn what he had discovered into a pathway that others might follow. Understandably, it went against his method whereby the onus was on the individual to discover, follow, practice, and experience all the aspects required to develop such wisdom. In the *Attadīpasutta* (SN 22.43, SuttaCentral, 2020, para. 2), he advises his students '… be your own island, your own refuge, with no other refuge. Let the teaching be your island and your refuge, with no other refuge'. He recounts that when he was at the Ajapālanigrodha, hesitating as to whether or not he should preach the Dhamma, Brahmā Sahampati appeared before him and asked him to teach. The Buddha agreed to this request. It is recorded in the *Brahmāyācanasutta* (SN 6.1, SuttaCentral, 2020, paras 1–16) that:

> *So, I have heard. At one time, when he was first awakened, the Buddha was staying near Uruvelā at the root of the goatherd's banyan tree on the bank of the Nerañjarā River.*
>
> *Then as he was in private retreat this thought came to his mind, "This principle I have discovered is deep, hard to see, hard to understand, peaceful, sublime, beyond the scope of reason, subtle, comprehensible to the astute. But people like attachment, they love it and enjoy it. It's hard for them to see this thing; that is, specific conditionality, dependent origination. It's also hard for them to see this thing; that is, the stilling of all activities, the letting go of all attachments, the ending of craving, fading away, cessation, extinguishment. And if I were to teach this principle, others might not understand me, which would be wearying and troublesome for me."* …
>
> … *And as the Buddha reflected like this, his mind inclined to remaining passive, not to teaching the Dhamma.*
>
> *Then Brahmā Sahampati, knowing what the Buddha was thinking, thought, "Oh my goodness! The world will be lost, the world will perish! For the mind of the Realized One, the perfected one, the fully awakened Buddha, inclines to remaining passive, not to teaching the Dhamma."*
>
> …
>
> *[then Brahmā Sahampati said: …]*
>
> *"Rise, hero! Victor in battle, leader of the caravan,*
>
> *Wander the world without obligation.*
>
> *Let the Blessed One teach the Dhamma!*
>
> *There will be those who understand!"*
>
> *Then the Buddha, understanding Brahmā's invitation, surveyed the world with the eye of a Buddha, because of his compassion for sentient beings. And the Buddha saw sentient beings with little dust in their eyes, and some with much dust in their eyes; with keen faculties and with weak faculties, with good qualities and with bad qualities, easy to teach and hard to teach. And some of them lived seeing the danger in the fault to do with the next world, while others did not.*
>
> *It's like a pool with blue water lilies, or pink or white lotuses. Some of them sprout and grow in the water without rising above it, thriving underwater. Some of them sprout and grow in the water reaching the water's surface. And some of them sprout and grow in the water but rise up above the water and stand with no water clinging to them.*
>
> *In the same way, the Buddha saw sentient beings with little dust in their eyes, and some with much dust in their eyes; with keen faculties and with weak faculties, with good qualities and with bad qualities, easy to teach and hard to teach. And some of them lived seeing the danger in the fault to do with the next world, while others did not.*

Over the 45 years that he went on to teach, he gave clear instructions about who could and could not teach his body of teachings. In the *Atthavasasutta* (AN 3.43, SuttaCentral, 2020), it is a simple matter of being one who has heard the teachings, has had direct, personal experience of the teachings and has understood their advantages. In the *Gotamakacetiyasutta* (AN 3.125, SuttaCentral, 2020, paras 1–4), it is recounted that:

> *On one occasion the Blessed One was staying near Vesālī at Gotamaka Shrine. There he addressed the monks, "Monks!"*
>
> *"Yes, lord," the monks responded.*
>
> *The Blessed One said, "It's through direct knowledge that I teach the Dhamma, not without direct knowledge. It's with a cause that I teach the Dhamma, not without a cause. It's with marvels that I teach the Dhamma, not without marvels. Because I teach the Dhamma through direct knowledge and not without direct knowledge, because I teach the Dhamma with a cause and not without a cause, because I teach the Dhamma with marvels and not without marvels, there is good reason for my instruction, good reason for my admonition. And that is enough for you to be content, enough for you to be gratified, enough for you to take joy that the Blessed One is rightly self-awakened, the Dhamma is well-taught by the Blessed One, and the community has practiced rightly."*
>
> *That is what the Blessed One said. Gratified, the monks delighted in the Blessed One's words. And while this explanation was being given, the ten-thousandfold cosmos quaked.*

In the *Atthavasasutta* (AN 3.43, SuttaCentral, 2020, para. 1), it is recorded that he extended this opportunity of teaching the Dhamma when one has developed in oneself this same wisdom, saying:

> *"Bhikkhus, when one sees three advantages, it is enough to teach others the Dhamma. What three?"*
>
> *"(1) The one who teaches the Dhamma experiences the meaning and the Dhamma. (2) The one who hears the Dhamma experiences the meaning and the Dhamma. (3) Both the one who teaches the Dhamma and the one who hears the Dhamma experience the meaning and the Dhamma. Seeing these three advantages, it is enough to teach others the Dhamma."*

From these discourses, it is possible to deduce that the Buddha gave weight to the personal, direct experience and understanding of the individual as a marker of their ability to teach.

4.4 Characteristics of a Skilful Teacher: *Pavīṇaupāya* by Skilful Means[3]

The idea of *pavīṇaupāya* by skilful means summarises the essence of the Buddha's pedagogical approach to the teaching of the Dhamma. In the EBTs and over time as the varieties of Buddhism as practised in Asia spread, it was as important to the Buddha how his ideas were taught as much as there being accurate transmission of *Buddha-Dhamma* core curriculum of the *cattari ariya saccani* Four Noble Truths and the *aṭṭhaṅgikaṃ maggaṃ* Noble Eightfold Path (see Appendix A and C). Whether a monk or a lay teacher, the Buddha encouraged those who were to begin the codification and dissemination processes to develop their *pavīṇaupāya* skilful means of

[3] A full discussion of the ideas found in this section can be found in Ma Rhea (2017).

teaching. Traditionally, in India and Asia, the Buddha's pedagogical methods used for developing *pavīṇaupāya* skilful means were passed on from monk and nun to their successor and these methods continue into the present. Over his teaching career, the Buddha was asked many times about what qualities a teacher should be able to demonstrate. Speaking to one of his monks, the *Udāyīsutta* (AN 5.159, SuttaCentral, 2020, para. 1) recounts:

> *I have heard that on one occasion the Blessed One was staying at Kosambi, in Ghosita's Park. Now at that time Ven. Udayin was sitting surrounded by a large assembly of householders, teaching the Dhamma. Ven. Ananda saw Ven. Udayin sitting surrounded by a large assembly of householders, teaching the Dhamma, and on seeing him went to the Blessed One. On arrival, he bowed down to the Blessed One and sat to one side. As he was sitting there he said to the Blessed One: "Ven. Udayin, lord, is sitting surrounded by a large assembly of householders, teaching the Dhamma."*

The Buddha's reply gives clear indication of the five qualities that should frame the preparations of a teacher of the Dhamma (AN 5.159, SuttaCentral, 2020, paras 2–7), saying:

> *"It's not easy to teach the Dhamma to others, Ananda. The Dhamma should be taught to others only when five qualities are established within the person teaching. Which five?"*
> *"[1] The Dhamma should be taught with the thought, 'I will speak step-by-step.'"*
> *"[2] The Dhamma should be taught with the thought, 'I will speak explaining the sequence [of cause & effect].'"*
> *"[3] The Dhamma should be taught with the thought, 'I will speak out of compassion.'"*
> *"[4] The Dhamma should be taught with the thought, 'I will speak not for the purpose of material reward.'"*
> *"[5] The Dhamma should be taught with the thought, 'I will speak without hurting myself or others.'"*
> *"It's not easy to teach the Dhamma to others, Ananda. The Dhamma should be taught to others only when these five qualities are established within the person teaching."*

He established the concept of a teacher as *kalyāṇamitta* good friend. In the *Kalyāṇamittasutta* (SN 3.18, SuttaCentral, 2020, paras 7–9) in a teaching he gave at Sāvatthī to King Pasenadi, the Buddha explains this key concept:

> *"... by relying on me as a good friend, sentient beings who are liable to rebirth, old age, and death, to sorrow, lamentation, pain, sadness, and distress are freed from all these things. This is another way to understand how good friends are the whole of the spiritual life."*
>
> *"So, great king, you should train like this: 'I will have good friends, companions, and associates.' That's how you should train."*
>
> *"When you have good friends, companions, and associates, you should live supported by one thing: diligence in skilful qualities."*

He also established, by example, the importance of having good conduct. In one of the longer *Suttas*, the *Brahmāyusutta* (MN 91, SuttaCentral, 2020), the Buddha is assessed by a highly respected Brahmin, Brahmāyu, who had mastered the Vedic curriculum. According to the 32 marks of a great man recognised in the Vedic tradition, the Brahmin Brahmāyu wants to see for himself whether the Buddha possesses these 32 marks because he recognised that if the Buddha had these 32 marks, he would make an important contribution to the spiritual development of all sentient beings, saying, '… if he [the Buddha] goes forth from the lay life to homelessness, he becomes a perfected one, a fully awakened Buddha, who draws back the veil from the world' (MN 91, SuttaCentral, 2020, para. 6). The Buddha was recognised as having the required marks through this sort of thorough assessment, such was the advanced state of programmes of spiritual development at the time of the Buddha and the Brahmin Brahmāyu.

In addition to developing wisdom through experiential understanding, having the five qualities one should have and undertaking the preparations one should make to be a teacher, being a *kalyāṇamitta* good friend, and being established in good conduct, the Buddha also taught his Sangha and lay followers many methods to teach the *Buddha Dhamma*. For example, the Buddha recommends that a teacher know when to be firm and when to be expansive. Bhikkhuni Ayya Khema (1988) explains that the concept of the *kalyāṇamitta* also encompasses being a teacher who is a reliable guide, giving true directions and she draws on the Buddha's discussion with a horse trainer to highlight the different methods that might be necessary for a teacher to use. The *Kesisutta* (AN 4.111, SuttaCentral, 2020, paras 1–13) records the teaching in this manner:

> *Then Kesi the horse trainer went up to the Buddha, bowed, and sat down to one side. The Buddha said to him, "Kesi, you're known as a horse trainer. Just how do you guide a horse in training?"*
>
> *"Sir, I guide a horse in training sometimes gently, sometimes harshly, and sometimes both gently and harshly."*
>
> *"Kesi, what do you do with a horse in training that doesn't follow these forms of training?"*
>
> *"In that case, sir, I kill it. Why is that? So that I don't disgrace my profession."*
>
> *"But sir, the Buddha is the supreme guide for those who wish to train. Just how do you guide a person in training?"*
>
> *"Kesi, I guide a person in training sometimes gently, sometimes harshly, and sometimes both gently and harshly."*
>
> *"The gentle way is this: 'This is good conduct by way of body, speech, and mind. This is the result of good conduct by way of body, speech, and mind. This is life as a god. This is life as a human.'"*
>
> *"The harsh way is this: 'This is bad conduct by way of body, speech, and mind. This is the result of bad conduct by way of body, speech, and mind. This is life in hell. This is life as an animal. This is life as a ghost.'"*
>
> *"The both gentle and harsh way is this: 'This is good conduct … this is bad conduct …'"*
>
> *"Sir, what do you do with a person in training who doesn't follow these forms of training?"*
>
> *"In that case, Kesi, I kill them."*

"Sir, it's not appropriate for the Buddha to kill living creatures. And yet you say you kill them."

"It's true, Kesi, it's not appropriate for a Realized One to kill living creatures. But when a person in training doesn't follow any of these forms of training, the Realised One doesn't think they're worth advising or instructing, and neither do their sensible spiritual companions. For it is death in the training of the noble one when the Realised One doesn't think they're worth advising or instructing, and neither do their sensible spiritual companions."

In the *Saddhasutta*, (AN 5.38, SuttaCentral, 2020), when speaking to clansmen, the Buddha explains, by his use of figurative language, that a teacher first and foremost must have confidence in the *Dhamma.* The word *saddhaññeva* implies having confidence in something, in this case, the Buddha's teachings, but with an important distinction; in the Buddha's philosophy of education, *saddha* faith arises through personal, experiential conviction rather than through simply believing something because it has been told to them. The Buddha explains the impact of one who has confidence in one's experiences of the development of their inner wisdom (AN 5.38, SuttaCentral, 2020, paras 3–5), saying:

"Just as at a crossroads on level ground, a great banyan tree becomes the resort for birds all around, so the clansman endowed with faith becomes the resort for many people: for bhikkhus, bhikkhunīs, male lay followers, and female lay followers."

A large tree with a mighty trunk,
branches, leaves, and fruit,
firm roots, and bearing fruit,
is a support for many birds.
Having flown across the sky,
the birds resort to this delightful base:
those in need of shade partake of its shade;
those needing fruit enjoy its fruit.
Just so, when a person is virtuous,
endowed with faith,
of humble manner, compliant,
gentle, welcoming, soft,
those in the world who are fields of merit—
devoid of lust and hatred,
devoid of delusion, taintless—
resort to such a person.
They teach him the Dhamma
that dispels all suffering,
having understood which
the taintless one here attains Nibbāna.

4.5 Characteristics of a Good Student

The next section moves to consideration of what we know about what is expected of the student, follower, learner, of how learning was conducted, and how a student was expected to behave. While the focus of this book is about the Buddha's way of educating for the development of wisdom through its examination of his teaching career, pedagogical approach and his core curriculum, it would be remiss not to provide an insight into what was expected of the student learner of this path. The Buddha, for example, in the *Sāriputtasutta* (AN 3.33, SuttaCentral, 2020, para. 2 in *Pāḷi* and English trans.), reflects in this famous phrase that:

> *Etassa, bhagavā, kālo, etassa, sugata, kālo yaṃ bhagavā saṅkhittenapi dhammaṃ deseyya, vitthārenapi dhammaṃ deseyya, saṅkhittavitthārenapi dhammaṃ deseyya. Bhavissanti dhammassa aññātāro"ti.*
>
> *"I can teach the Dhamma briefly; I can teach the Dhamma in detail; I can teach the Dhamma both briefly and in detail. It is those who can understand that are rare."*

He explains the eight qualities that he looks for in someone seeking to learn from him. In the *Puṇṇiyasutta* (AN 8.82, SuttaCentral, 2020, paras 2–4), Puṇṇiya asks the Buddha:

> *"Sir, what is the cause, what is the reason why sometimes the Realised One feels inspired to teach, and other times not?"*

The Buddha replies:

> *"Puṇṇiya, when a mendicant has faith but doesn't approach, the Realised One doesn't feel inspired to teach. But when a mendicant has faith and approaches, the Realised One feels inspired to teach.*
>
> *When a mendicant has faith and approaches, but doesn't pay homage …*
>
> *they pay homage, but don't ask questions …*
>
> *they ask questions, but don't lend an ear …*
>
> *they lend an ear, but don't remember the teaching they've heard …*
>
> *they remember the teaching they've heard, but don't reflect on the meaning of the teachings they've remembered …*
>
> *they reflect on the meaning of the teachings they've remembered, but, having understood the meaning and the teaching, they don't practice accordingly. The Realised One doesn't feel inspired to teach.*
>
> *But when a mendicant has faith, approaches, pays homage, asks questions, lends an ear, remembers the teachings, reflects on the meaning, and practices accordingly, the Realised One feels inspired to teach. When someone has these eight qualities, the Realised One feels totally inspired to teach."*

There are many examples given of the sorts of qualities and characteristics that the Buddha valued in his students. In the *Sattamavagga* (AN 1.258–267, SuttaCentral, 2020, paras 1–10) he praises the following nuns, saying:

"The foremost of my laywomen in first going for refuge is Sujātā Seniyadhītā.
... as a donor is Visākhā, Migāra's mother.
... who are very learned is Khujjuttarā.
... who dwell in love is Sāmāvatī.
... who practice absorption is Uttarānandamātā.
... who give fine things is Suppavāsā Koliyadhītā.
... who care for the sick is the laywoman Suppiyā.
... who have experiential confidence is Kātiyānī.
... who are intimate is the householder Nakula's mother.
... whose confidence is based on oral transmission is the laywoman Kāḷī of Kuraraghara."

The last of these, ... '*Anussavappasannānaṃ yadidaṃ kāḷī upāsikā kuraragharikā"ti.* confidence based on oral transmission' speaks to the confidence people had in the reliability of the oral transmission of the Buddha's words, tested by experience giving veracity to the teachings.

4.6 The *Majjhima Patipada* Middle Way as Pedagogy

This discussion of the Buddha's pedagogy returns to what was introduced in Chap. 2 as the foundation of the Buddha's pedagogical approach, the *Majjhima Patipada* Middle Way approach to the development of wisdom. Beare and Slaughter (1993) provide encouragement for a thorough examination of the inclusion of Buddhist teachings into discussions about education and the future. Beare and Slaughter suggest that it is seriously flawed to leave the question of human motives unaddressed in education. They say,

> *It is our observation that when low-level human motives such as fear, greed and hostility become associated with powerful technologies, the result is indeed a long running disaster. But when high motives such as selfless love, stewardship and what Buddhists call 'loving kindness' come into play, there are interesting consequences.* (p. 166)

The question of how to teach such higher motives through the development of a student's capacity for the emergence of wisdom is fully developed in the Buddha's approach of the *Majjhima Patipada* Middle Way. In this final section of Chap. 4, I will introduce the key aspects of this approach and in the following chapter (Chap. 5, this edition), I will examine some of the pedagogical techniques that the Buddha used and reflect on the ways that these techniques can anchor the Buddha's core curriculum into the present and future eras in formal schooling. As shown in Fig. 4.2, the *sikkhāpana* pedagogy of the *Majjhima Patipada* Middle Way includes three elements: *pariyatti* (theoretical knowledge, also referred to as 'learning the wording of the doctrine'), *paṭipatti* ('practising it' [the doctrine]), and *paṭivedha* (understanding of experiences, also referred to as 'penetrating it') (Ven Nyanatiloka, 1988, p. 150) towards the realising its goal of attaining wisdom (Fig. 4.2).

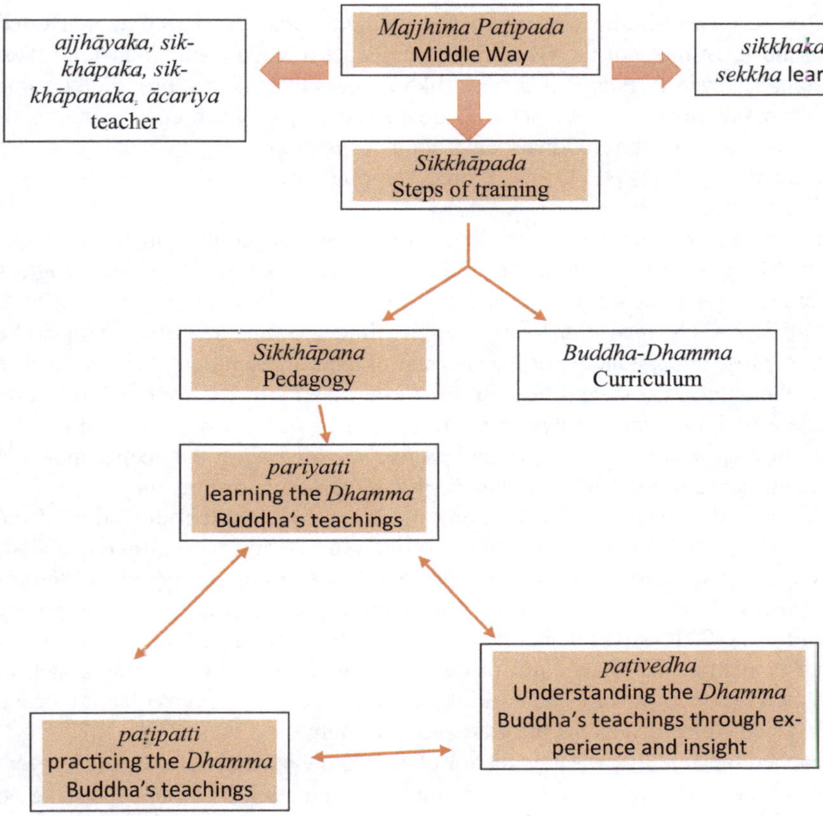

Fig. 4.2 Elements of the Buddha's pedagogy: the *Majjhima Patipada* Middle Way approach

The concept of gradual development is a core to his approach. Ven Nyanatiloka (1988, p. 169) explains this approach in an explanation titled 'Progress of the Disciple', saying:

> *Gradual development of the Eightfold Path in the progress of the disciple: In many suttas occurs an identical passage that outlines the gradual course of development in the progress of the disciple. There it is shown how this development takes place gradually, and in conformity with laws, from the very first hearing of the doctrine, and from germinating faith and dim comprehension, up to the final realisation of deliverance.*

The process begins with the first element of the *sikkhāpana* pedagogy, *pariyatti* hearing and learning the Buddha's teachings. This is followed by the second element of the *sikkhāpana* pedagogy, guiding the student to *paṭipatti* practising the methods explained by the Buddha to achieve personal, tacit understanding. The third element of the *sikkhāpana* pedagogy, *paṭivedha*, guides the student to use insight and discernment to penetrate and understand the deeper meaning of the teachings. This *sikkhāpana* pedagogy gives rise to confidence, spoken of as 'faith', in the Buddha's

Majjhima Patipada Middle Way approach causing the learner to become motivated to hear and learn more of the Dhamma, practice its methods, and deepening their understanding even further. It is a spiral-like process that circles through the same teachings many times and understanding deepens over years, and up to a final realisation of wisdom that the Buddha speaks about as *nibbāna* enlightenment (Buddhadatta Mahathera, 1958, p. 143; for further elaboration of this important term, see SuttaCentral, 2020).

The process also employs scaffolded instruction, as outlined in the previous sections. Many *Suttas* are about the Buddha tailoring his teaching to the progress of the student. Over the 45-year period of his teaching life, as discussed in Chap. 2 (this edition), he returned to the same people, time and time and time again, so he had a very close understanding of the progress of their development, because he was close to them and they sought him out for further learning. His approach relies on the student finding balance between the three aspects of his *sikkhāpana* pedagogy, cycling through *pariyatti*, *paṭipatti*, and *paṭivedha* penetrating the deeper meaning and making sense of the Dhamma then beginning the cycle over again.

As discussed in Chap. 3 (this edition), the arrangement and codification of the *Majjhima Patipada* Middle Way approach follow a similar approach to that of modern knowledge management techniques for professional learning promoted by Nonaka and Takeuchi (1995). There are also many familiar elements in the contemporary work of Smith (2012/2019) where he examines the nature of pedagogy in informal learning contexts. The connection of the importance of pedagogical approach to what would now be known as 'soft-skills development' was a central feature of the Buddha's engagement with people wherever he taught.

As a teacher, the Buddha was a generator of new knowledge about the development of wisdom. He was selecting and organising the content all the time, depending on the question asked him by a student. He was, simultaneously developing a teachable language to support his concepts because this language did not exist prior to his teaching of his experiential understandings as a *samma sambuddha* enlightened Buddha who was able to teach what he had learned. He was adapting and refining the meaning of words and concepts that were familiar to his students from the Rig Veda, the Upanishads, and the Brahminical education tradition, and he was adapting it in conversation with Jains and Brahmans, and other people at the time, but particularly with Jains and Brahmins, while developing his own ideas about what these words meant within his education philosophy for the development of wisdom. Over time, he developed a language to support his teaching ideas while also assessing learner readiness, aspects that would be familiar to the contemporary classroom teacher or lecturer.

In Bloom's (1956, 1976, 1994) cognitive learning sense, the Buddha's approach in the *pariyatti* phase establishes knowledge and comprehension, Bloom's first two levels. The Buddha standardises words and phrases, across in many different *Suttas*, reproduced over and over again. It means that the student can have some confidence that it is what he said because it was reproduced so many times. He uses a lot of repetition and numbering as techniques (to be discussed in more detail in a later section).

He embeds cognitive understanding of his teaching through repetition. In a practice established during his lifetime and continued over these past 2,500 years, he developed an approach to memorisation of his teachings through a concept of cooperative learning. Similar to the modern concept of teachers having communities of learning to support their ongoing professional development, these communities shaped as they were by the oral tradition, formed around memorisation of the Dhamma. Modern communities of learning can rely on the printed word, using their collaborations to deepen understanding of the key ideas within the profession of teaching without also having to memorise key teachings. The teachers of the Buddha's time had to undertake both aspects: memorisation and deepening of their pedagogical and content understandings together during those times when the Buddha was teaching in other parts of the region and after his passing.

In terms of cognitive learning, in Bloom's sense, the *paṭipatti* phase reflects the application of the instruction. This is the point where the student starts to apply what they have been taught and this is very much the experiential aspect that is so important to the Buddha's approach. Similar to Indigenous and other traditionally-oriented approaches to education, anything observed, heard, or taught has to be experienced. It is a very internal process of learning, that embeds the learning in a way that is personal and tacit (Polanyi, 1958/1998). A pedagogical approach that is less well understood in the formal learning classroom that is developed across the world, the Buddha's approach adopted by teachers of the Dhamma up to the present day actively encourages, indeed requires that the student practice what they have been taught. Within this approach, the differentiation of practice instruction, according to need, is given in the first phase of *pariyatti*. The Buddha remarked many times about the importance of clear instructions for practice. He advised his Sangha, the first teachers of his method, to follow this same path because they could not teach what they had not experienced for themselves. He had confidence in what he was teaching because he'd experienced it. He was also able to tailor the practices to the needs and abilities of the individual learner.

A remarkable and enduring feature of his method, emphasised in the *paṭipatti* phase was that a student should believe nothing that was being taught but test each method of practice according to need and, through undergoing the third *paṭivedha* phase, penetrate the deeper meaning of the teachings, thus progressing on the path to wisdom. As mentioned previously, his approach determined that if the student heard the teachings, practised them, and then delved into what had been experienced to attain deeper understanding, then confidence in the teachings would arise. It was this confidence rather than uncritical acceptance of what was being taught that would convince the student to return to the teacher for more instruction.

The premise of the Buddha's pedagogy is that the learner is encouraged to follow this gradual path, hearing; practising virtue, sense restraint, mindfulness and alertness, abandoning what is unskilful and practising what is skilful moment by moment. In the next chapter, I will delve more deeply into the methods and techniques that the Buddha used and taught others how to use to teach the Buddha-Dhamma.

References

Suttas

SuttaCentral. (2020). Aṅguttara Nikāya 1.258–267. *Sattamavagga* Seventh. [Bhikkhu Sujato, Trans.]. Retrieved December 31, 2020 from https://suttacentral.net/an1.258-267/en/sujato. Translated for SuttaCentral by Bhikkhu Sujato, 2018. Dedicated to the public domain via Creative Commons Zero (CC0). You are encouraged to copy, reproduce, adapt, alter, or otherwise make use of this translation in any way you wish. Attribution is appreciated but not legally required.

SuttaCentral. (2020). Saṃyutta Nikāya 25. *Okkantasaṁyutta.* Retrieved December 31, 2020 from https://suttacentral.net/sn25.

SuttaCentral (2020). Aṅguttara Nikāya 3.125. *Gotamakacetiyasutta* At Gotamaka Shrine. [Bhikkhu Thanissaro, Trans.]. Retrieved December 31, 2020 from https://suttacentral.net/an3.125/en/thanissaro. Translated from the Pāḷi by Thanissaro Bhikkhu. The text of this page is licensed under a Creative Commons Attribution-NonCommercial 4.0 International License. To view a copy of the license, visit http://creativecommons.org/licenses/by-nc/4.0/. Documents linked from this page may be subject to other restrictions. Transcribed from a file provided by the translator. Access to Insight (Legacy Edition), 30 November 2013, http://www.accesstoinsight.org/. Prepared for SuttaCentral by Gabriel Laera and Ayya Vimala.

SuttaCentral. (2020). Aṅguttara Nikāya 3.33. *Sāriputtasutta.* Sāriputta. Retrieved December 31, 2020 from https://suttacentral.net/an3.33/pli/ms. Pāḷi text from the Mahāsaṅgīti Tipiṭaka Buddhavasse 2500: World Tipiṭaka Edition in Roman Script. Edited and published by The M.L. Maniratana Bunnag Dhamma Society Fund, 2005. Based on the digital edition of the Chaṭṭha Saṅgāyana published by the Vipassana Re-search Institute, with corrections and proofreading by the Dhamma Society.

SuttaCentral. (2020). Aṅguttara Nikāya 3.33. *Sāriputtasutta.* Sāriputta. [Bhikkhu Bodhi, Trans.]. Retrieved December 31, 2020 from https://suttacentral.net/an3.33/en/bodhi. The Numerical Discourses of the Buddha (Wisdom Publications, 2012). This excerpt from The Numerical Discourses of the Buddha by Bhikkhu Bodhi is licensed under a Creative Commons Attribution-NonCommercial-NoDerivs 3.0 Unported License. Based on the work The Numerical Discourses of the Buddha at Wisdom Publications. Permissions beyond the scope of this license may be available at Wisdom Publications. Prepared for SuttaCentral by Blake Walsh.

SuttaCentral. (2020). Aṅguttara Nikāya 3.43. *Atthavasasutta* Advantages. [Bhikkhu Bodhi, Trans.]. Retrieved December 31, 2020 from https://suttacentral.net/an3.43/en/bodhi. The Numerical Discourses of the Buddha (Wisdom Publications, 2012). This excerpt from The Numerical Discourses of the Buddha by Bhikkhu Bodhi is licensed under a Creative Commons Attribution—Non Commercial—No Derivs 3.0 Unported License. Based on the work The Numerical Discourses of the Buddha at Wisdom Publications. Permissions beyond the scope of this license may be available at Wisdom Publications. Prepared for SuttaCentral by Blake Walsh.

SuttaCentral. (2020). Aṅguttara Nikāya 4.111. *Kesisutta* With Kesi. [Bhikkhu Sujato, Trans.]. Retrieved December 31, 2020 from https://suttacentral.net/an4.111/en/sujato. Translated for SuttaCentral by Bhikkhu Sujato, 2018. Dedicated to the public domain via Creative Commons Zero (CC0). You are encouraged to copy, reproduce, adapt, alter, or otherwise make use of this translation in any way you wish. Attribution is appreciated but not legally required.

SuttaCentral. (2020). Aṅguttara Nikāya 5.159. *Udāyīsutta* About Udayin [Bhikkhu Thanissaro, Trans.]. Retrieved December 31, 2020 from https://suttacentral.net/an5.159/en/thanissaro. Translated from the Pāḷi by Thanissaro Bhikkhu. The text of this page is licensed under a Creative Commons Attribution-NonCommercial 4.0 International License. To view a copy of the license, visit http://creativecommons.org/licenses/by-nc/4.0/. Documents linked from this page may be subject to other restrictions. Transcribed from a file provided by the translator. Access to Insight (Legacy Edition), 30 November 2013, http://www.accesstoinsight.org/. Prepared for SuttaCentral by Gabriel Laera and Ayya Vimala.

SuttaCentral. (2020). Aṅguttara Nikāya 5.38. *Saddhasutta* Faith. [Bhikkhu Bodhi, Trans.]. Retrieved December 31, 2020 from https://suttacentral.net/an5.38/en/bodhi. The Numerical Discourses of the Buddha (Wisdom Publications, 2012). This excerpt from The Numerical Discourses of the Buddha by Bhikkhu Bodhi is licensed under a Creative Commons Attribution—Non Commercial—No Derivs 3.0 Unported License. Based on the work The Numerical Discourses of the Buddha at Wisdom Publications. Permissions beyond the scope of this license may be available at Wisdom Publications. Prepared for SuttaCentral by Blake Walsh.

SuttaCentral. (2020). Aṅguttara Nikāya 8.19. *Pahārādasutta* Pahārāda. [Bhikkhu Bodhi, Trans.]. Retrieved December 31, 2020 from https://suttacentral.net/an8.19/en/bodhi. The Numerical Discourses of the Buddha (Wisdom Publications, 2012). This excerpt from The Numerical Discourses of the Buddha by Bhikkhu Bodhi is licensed under a Creative Commons Attribution—Non Commercial - No Derivs 3.0 Unported License. Based on the work The Numerical Discourses of the Buddha at Wisdom Publications. Permissions beyond the scope of this license may be available at Wisdom Publications. Prepared for SuttaCentral by Blake Walsh.

SuttaCentral. (2020). Aṅguttara Nikāya 8.82. *Puṇṇiyasutta* With Puṇṇiya. [Bhikkhu Sujato, Trans.]. Retrieved December 31, 2020 from https://suttacentral.net/an8.82/en/sujato. Translated for SuttaCentral by Bhikkhu Sujato, 2018. Dedicated to the public domain via Creative Commons Zero (CC0). You are encouraged to copy, reproduce, adapt, alter, or otherwise make use of this translation in any way you wish. Attribution is appreciated but not legally required.

SuttaCentral. (2020). *Dhammapada*. Retrieved December 31, 2020 from https://suttacentral.net/dhp.

SuttaCentral. (2020). Majjhima Nikāya 20. *Vitakkasaṇṭhānasutta*. The Removal of Distracting Thoughts. [Bhikkhu Bodhi, Trans.]. Retrieved December 31, 2020 from https://suttacentral.net/mn20/en/bodhi. The Middle Length Discourses of the Buddha (Wisdom Publications, 2009). This excerpt from The Middle Length Discourses of the Buddha by Bhikkhu Bodhi is licensed under a Creative Commons Attribution—Non Commercial—No Derivs 3.0 Unported License. Based on the work The Middle Length Discourses of the Buddha at Wisdom Publications. Permissions beyond the scope of this license may be available at Wisdom Publications. Prepared for SuttaCentral by Blake Walsh.

SuttaCentral. (2020). Majjhima Nikāya 28. *Mahāhatthipadopamasutta* The Greater Discourse on the Simile of the Elephant's Footprint. [Bhikkhu Bodhi, Trans.]. Retrieved December 31, 2020 from https://suttacentral.net/mn28/en/bodhi. The Middle Length Discourses of the Buddha (Wisdom Publications, 2009). This excerpt from The Middle Length Discourses of the Buddha by Bhikkhu Bodhi is licensed under a Creative Commons Attribution—Non Commercial—No Derivs 3.0 Unported License. Based on the work The Middle Length Discourses of the Buddha at Wisdom Publications. Permissions beyond the scope of this license may be available at Wisdom Publications. Prepared for SuttaCentral by Blake Walsh.

SuttaCentral. (2020). Majjhima Nikāya 38. *Mahātaṇhāsaṅkhayasutta* The Greater Discourse on the Destruction of Craving. [Bhikkhu Bodhi, Trans.]. Retrieved December 31, 2020 from https://suttacentral.net/mn38/en/bodhi. The Middle Length Discourses of the Buddha (Wisdom Publications, 2009). This excerpt from The Middle Length Discourses of the Buddha by Bhikkhu Bodhi is licensed under a Creative Commons Attribution—Non Commercial—No Derivs 3.0 Unported License. Based on the work The Middle Length Discourses of the Buddha at Wisdom Publications. Permissions beyond the scope of this license may be available at Wisdom Publications. Prepared for SuttaCentral by Blake Walsh.

SuttaCentral. (2020). Majjhima Nikāya 91. *Brahmāyusutta* With Brahmāyu. [Bhikkhu Sujato, Trans.]. Retrieved December 31, 2020 from https://suttacentral.net/mn91/en/sujato. Translated for SuttaCentral by Bhikkhu Sujato, 2018. Dedicated to the public domain via Creative Commons Zero (CC0). You are encouraged to copy, reproduce, adapt, alter, or otherwise make use of this translation in any way you wish. Attribution is appreciated but not legally required.

SuttaCentral. (2020). Saṃyutta Nikāya 12.1. *Paṭiccasamuppādasutta* Dependent Origination. [Bhikkhu Bodhi, Trans]. Retrieved December 31, 2020 from https://suttacentral.net/sn12.1/en/bodhi. The Connected Discourses of the Buddha (Wisdom Publica-tions, 2000). This excerpt from The Connected Discourses of the Buddha by Bhikkhu Bodhi is licensed under a Creative Commons Attribution—Non Commercial—No Derivs 3.0 Un-ported License. Based on the work Connected Discourses of the Buddha at Wisdom Publications. Permissions beyond the scope of this license may be available at Wisdom Publications. Prepared for SuttaCentral by Blake Walsh.

SuttaCentral. (2020). Saṃyutta Nikāya 12.23. *Upanisasutta* Proximate Cause. [Bhikkhu Bodhi, Trans.]. Retrieved December 31, 2020 from https://suttacentral.net/sn12.23/en/bodhi. The Connected Discourses of the Buddha (Wisdom Publications, 2000). This excerpt from The Connected Discourses of the Buddha by Bhikkhu Bodhi is licensed under a Creative Commons Attribution—Non Commercial—No Derivs 3.0 Un-ported License. Based on the work Connected Discourses of the Buddha at Wisdom Publications. Permissions beyond the scope of this license may be available at Wisdom Publications. Prepared for SuttaCentral by Blake Walsh.

SuttaCentral. (2020). Saṃyutta Nikāya 18. *Rāhula Saṃyutta*. Retrieved December 31, 2020 from https://suttacentral.net/sn18.

SuttaCentral. (2020). Saṃyutta Nikāya 20.1–12. *Opamma Vagga*. [Bhikkhu Sujato, Trans.]. Retrieved December 31, 2020 from https://suttacentral.net/sn20-opammavagga. Translated for SuttaCentral by Bhikkhu Sujato, 2018. Dedicated to the public domain via Creative Commons Zero (CC0). You are encouraged to copy, reproduce, adapt, alter, or otherwise make use of this translation in any way you wish. Attribution is appreciated but not legally required.

SuttaCentral. (2020). Saṃyutta Nikāya 22.43. *Attadīpasutta* Be Your Own Island. [Bhikkhu Sujato, Trans.]. Retrieved December 31, 2020 from https://suttacentral.net/sn22.43/en/sujato. Translated for SuttaCentral by Bhikkhu Sujato, 2018. Dedicated to the public domain via Creative Commons Zero (CC0). You are encouraged to copy, reproduce, adapt, alter, or otherwise make use of this translation in any way you wish. Attribution is appreciated but not legally required.

SuttaCentral. (2020). Saṃyutta Nikāya 22.81. *Pālileyyasutta* Parileyya. [Bhikkhu Bodhi, Trans.]. Retrieved December 31, 2020 from https://suttacentral.net/sn22.81/en/bodhi. The Connected Discourses of the Buddha (Wisdom Publica-tions, 2000). This excerpt from The Connected Discourses of the Buddha by Bhikkhu Bodhi is licensed under a Creative Commons Attribution—Non Commercial—No Derivs 3.0 Un-ported License. Based on the work Connected Discourses of the Buddha at Wisdom Publications. Permissions beyond the scope of this license may be available at Wisdom Publications. Prepared for SuttaCentral by Blake Walsh.

SuttaCentral. (2020). Saṃyutta Nikāya 3.18. *Kalyāṇamittasutta* Good Friends. [Bhikkhu Sujato, Trans.]. Retrieved December 31, 2020 from https://suttacentral.net/sn3.18/en/sujato. Translated for SuttaCentral by Bhikkhu Sujato, 2018. Dedicated to the public domain via Creative Commons Zero (CC0). You are encouraged to copy, reproduce, adapt, alter, or otherwise make use of this translation in any way you wish. Attribution is appreciated but not legally required.

SuttaCentral. (2020). Saṃyutta Nikāya 36. *Vedanā Saṃyutta*. Retrieved December 31, 2020 from https://suttacentral.net/sn36.

SuttaCentral. (2020). Saṃyutta Nikāya 48. *Indriya Saṃyutta*. Retrieved December 31, 2020 from https://suttacentral.net/sn48.

SuttaCentral. (2020). Saṃyutta Nikāya 56.11. *Dhammacakkappavattanasutta* Setting in Motion the Wheel of the Dhamma. [Bhikkhu Bodhi, Trans.]. Retrieved December 31, 2020 from https://suttacentral.net/sn56.11/en/bodhi. The Connected Discourses of the Buddha (Wisdom Publications, 2000). This excerpt from The Connected Discourses of the Buddha by Bhikkhu Bodhi is licensed under a Creative Commons Attribution—Non Commercial—No Derivs 3.0 Un-ported License. Based on the work Connected Discourses of the Buddha at Wisdom Publications. Permissions beyond the scope of this license may be available at Wisdom Publications. Prepared for SuttaCentral by Blake Walsh.

SuttaCentral. (2020). Saṃyutta Nikāya 6.1. *Brahmāyācanasutta* The Appeal of Brahmā. [Bhikkhu Sujato, Trans.]. Retrieved December 31, 2020 from https://suttacentral.net/sn6.1/en/sujato. Translated for SuttaCentral by Bhikkhu Sujato, 2018. Dedicated to the public domain via Creative Commons Zero (CC0). You are encouraged to copy, reproduce, adapt, alter, or otherwise make use of this translation in any way you wish. Attribution is appreciated but not legally required.

Authored Texts

Beare, H., & Slaughter, R. (1993). *Education for the twenty-first century*. Routledge.

Bhikkhu Bodhi. (1980). *Transcendental dependent arising: A translation and exposition of the Upanisa Sutta*. Buddhist Publication Society.

Bhikkhu Thanissaro. (2010). *The ten perfections: A study guide*. Retrieved December 31, 2020 from Access to Insight. https://www.accesstoinsight.org/lib/study/perfections.html.

Bhikkhuni Ayya Khema. (1988). *Little dust in our eyes*. Sarvodaya Vishva Lekha.

Bloom, B. S. (1956). *Taxonomy of educational objectives, handbook I: The cognitive domain*. David McKay.

Bloom, B. S. (1976). *Human characteristics and school learning*. McGraw-Hill.

Bloom, B. S. (1994). Reflections on the development and use of the taxonomy. In L. W. Anderson, L. A. Sosniak, B. S. Bloom, & National Society for the Study of Education (Eds.), *Bloom's taxonomy: A forty-year retrospective* (pp. 1–8). National Society for the Study of Education.

Buddhadatta Mahathera, A. P. (1958). *Concise Pāḷi-English dictionary*. Singapore Buddhist Meditation Centre.

Buddhist Publication Society. (2020). *Buddhist Publication Society online library*. Retrieved December 31, 2020 from Buddhist Publication Society. https://www.bps.lk/index.php.

Gombrich, R. F. (2012). *Buddhist precept & practice* (1st ed.). Routledge.

Mayring, P. (2000). Qualitative content analysis. *Qualitative Methods in Various Disciplines, 1*(2), Article 20. https://doi.org/10.17169/fqs-1.2.1089.

Ma Rhea, Z. (2017). Buddhist pedagogy in teacher education: Cultivating wisdom by skillful means. *Asia-Pacific Journal of Teacher Education*, 1–18. Online available at https://doi.org/10.1080/1359866X.2017.1399984.

Nonaka, I., & Takeuchi, H. (1995). *The knowledge creating company: How Japanese companies create the dynamics of innovation*. Oxford University Press.

Pāḷi Text Society. (2020). *Pāli canon in English translation*. Pāḷi Text Society. Retrieved December 31, 2020 from Pāḷi Text Society. http://www.pāḷitext.com/pāḷitext/tipitaka.htm.

Polanyi, M. (1958/1998). *Personal knowledge: Towards a post critical philosophy*. Routledge.

Smith, M. K. (2012/2019). *What is pedagogy? A definition and discussion*. Retrieved December 31, 2020 from Infed.org. https://infed.org/mobi/what-is-pedagogy/.

Sujato, & Brahmali, Bhikkhu. (2015). *The authenticity of the early buddhist texts*. Chroniker Press. https://ocbs.org/wp-content/uploads/2015/09/authenticity.pdf.

SuttaCentral. (2020a). *Early Buddhist texts, translations, and parallels*. Retrieved December 31, 2020 from SuttaCentral. https://suttacentral.net/.

SuttaCentral. (2020b). *Nibbāna*. Retrieved December 31, 2020 from SuttaCentral. https://suttacentral.net/define/nibbāna.

Ven Nyanatiloka. (1988). *Buddhist dictionary: Manual of Buddhist terms and doctrine* (4th ed., Reprinted). Buddhist Publication Society.

Chapter 5
The Gradual Path for the Development of Wisdom

Abstract The final chapter turns to an analysis of the teaching strategies and pedagogical techniques employed by the Buddha to teach the *Buddha-Dhamma* core curriculum of the *cattari ariya saccani* Four Noble Truths and the *aṭṭhaṅgikaṃ maggaṃ* Noble Eightfold Path found in the *Tipitaka* Buddhist Canon (see Appendix C). It will tease out the Buddha's *Majjhima Patipada* Middle Way methods and examine the importance of these for modern education, in particular the experiential element. I will conclude with a discussion of the key elements of the Buddha's education theory, their importance, and relevance for modern education.

Keywords Teaching strategies · Teacher pedagogical techniques · Learner engagement practices · Teaching for wisdom · *Majjhima Patipada* Middle Way pedagogy

5.1 Methods for Teaching the *Buddha-Dhamma* Core Curriculum

The Buddha's education theory is founded on the concept of gradual development 'from the very first hearing of the doctrine, and from germinating faith and dim comprehension, up to the final realization of deliverance' (Ven Nyanatiloka, 1988, p. 169). There are many references to the Buddha's confirmation of this being the way to teach, 'little by little'. For example, in the *Dutiyakālasutta* (AN 4.147, SuttaCentral, 2020, paras. 1–3), the Buddha explains this concept, saying:

> *"Mendicants, when these four times are rightly developed and progressed, they gradually lead to the ending of defilements. What four? A time for listening to the teaching, a time for discussing the teaching, a time for serenity, and a time for discernment."*
>
> *"It's like when it rains heavily on a mountain top, and the water flows downhill to fill the hollows, crevices, and creeks. As they become full, they fill up the pools. The pools fill up the lakes, the lakes fill up the streams, and the streams fill up the rivers. And as the rivers become full, they fill up the ocean."*
>
> *"In the same way, when these four times are rightly developed and progressed, they gradually lead to the ending of defilements."*

Z. M. Diamond, *Gautama Buddha*, https://doi.org/10.1007/978-981-16-1765-2_5

The Buddha's *Majjhima Patipada* Middle Way method is taught in three stages, through direct teaching of *pariyatti* theoretical knowledge (also referred to as 'learning the doctrine'), providing techniques for *paṭipatti* 'practicing it' [the doctrine], and helping students in *paṭivedha* the understanding of their experiences (also referred to as 'penetrating it') (Ven Nyanatiloka, 1988, p. 150). This approach is spirallic, akin to the modern idea of knowledge management proposed by Nonaka (1994), adding a dimension of targeted experiential practice by the student. In the following sections, I will examine each aspect of the *Majjhima Patipada* Middle Way to discuss the pedagogical methods used, the teaching and learning focus, the teacher's pedagogical techniques and the learner's engagement practices with reference to the EBTs (SuttaCentral, 2020).

5.2 Stage 1: *Pariyatti* Learning the Doctrine

The first aspect of the method used by the Buddha and taught by him to the *Sangha* of *bhikkhus* monks and *bhikkhunis* nuns and also lay people who went on to arrange, codify, and disseminate his teachings over the past 2,500 years is *pariyatti* theoretical knowledge, also referred to as 'learning the doctrine' (Ven Nyanatiloka, 1988, p. 150). Bhikkhu Bodhi (1999, p. 2) explains that:

> *To follow the Noble Eightfold Path is a matter of practice rather than intellectual knowledge, but to apply the path correctly it has to be properly understood. In fact, right understanding of the path is itself a part of the practice. It is a facet of right view, the first path factor, the forerunner and guide for the rest of the path. Thus, though initial enthusiasm might suggest that the task of intellectual comprehension may be shelved as a bothersome distraction, mature consideration reveals it to be quite essential to ultimate success in the practice.*

It was 'a time for listening to the teaching [and] a time for discussing the teaching' (*Dutiyakālasutta*, AN 4.147, SuttaCentral, 2020, para. 1). For teaching his students approaches to *Pariyatti* learning the doctrine, the Buddha used two strategies (Table 5.1) that would be familiar to the modern classroom teacher: direct instruction and teaching for understanding.

Table 5.1 Teaching strategies and techniques for *Pariyatti* learning the doctrine

Teaching strategies	Teacher pedagogical techniques	Learner engagement practices
Explicit Instruction • Cognitive clarity • Verbal clarity Teaching for understanding	Standardisation of words and phrases Numbers and Mnemonics Analogy and figurative language	Co-operative learning • Memorisation • Group recital

The *Suttas* provide many examples of two teaching strategies that the Buddha commonly used: explicit instruction and teaching for understanding. This first stage of *Pariyatti* is most closely aligned to Bloom's Remember and Understand categories of cognitive development (Krathwohl et al., 2001) involving cognitive processes such as recognising, recalling, interpreting, inferring, and comparing.

5.2.1 Explicit Instruction

Killen (2013) explains that '... explicit instruction usually refers to whole class expository teaching techniques ... they are teacher-centred approaches in which the teacher delivers academic content in a highly structured format that directs the activities of the learners and maintains the focus on academic achievement' (p. 131). For the Buddha, this strategy became an effective, efficient, and appealing method for teaching people ways of *pariyatti* learning the doctrine. I will discuss two notable examples of the Buddha's approach to explicit instruction that carefully guided the student to be able to lay the foundation for the understanding of their experiences, his cognitive and verbal clarity.

The Buddha's cognitive clarity is evident across the *Suttas.* In the *Sīhasutta* (AN 8.12, SuttaCentral, 2020), for example, the Buddha is challenged about a number of aspects of his teachings by General Sīha who was a follower of the Jains. Here we can see a number of aspects of the Buddha's cognitive clarity: logical sequencing, providing explanation of what he meant by the main ideas step-by-step in ways that would be understood by the General, addressed his questions, and summarised his main ideas after he had checked that General Sīha had understood (AN 8.12, SuttaCentral, 2020, para. 33), for example:

> *... the Buddha taught Sīha step by step, with a talk on giving, ethical conduct, and heaven. He explained the drawbacks of sensual pleasures, so sordid and corrupt, and the benefit of renunciation. And when the Buddha knew that Sīha's mind was ready, pliable, rid of hindrances, joyful, and confident he explained the special teaching of the Buddhas: suffering, its origin, its cessation, and the path. Just as a clean cloth rid of stains would properly absorb dye, in that very seat the stainless, immaculate vision of the Dhamma arose in General Sīha: "Everything that has a beginning has an end."*

His verbal clarity was also evident. This aspect, together with cognitive clarity and his communication style all speak to his skills in oratory. As was discussed in Chap. 2, the world was an oral world in the time of the Buddha, and there are many aspects of oratory that have become less obvious in the literate world. Even so, the skilled orator is still able to move people emotionally and spiritually in the contemporary world. Indigenous people in many parts of the world continue to be raised in families and communities where orality is more common than the written word (Ma Rhea, 2012) and modern schooling often misses the subtleties and nuances of oratorical techniques that were so effectively employed by the Buddha. His verbal clarity was captured well in the following example where he explicitly teaches about suffering *dukkha* and the path to the cessation of suffering *dukkha.* While some of his verbal clarity can be attributed to those who assembled, organised, and codified his teachings, within the teachings there remains an essence of his oratorical skills. In this next example, he is teaching the methods for practising meditation, a key element in the experiential aspect of the *Majjhima Patipada* Middle Way approach. Elements of this teaching appear in many other teachings, but here in the *Satipaṭṭhānasutta* (MN 10, SuttaCentral, 2020), he brings all the elements together, demonstrating that this is a well-planned teaching based on his experiential understanding of the method. He is clear about what must be practised and how and provides enough information, based on this experience to guide the student into self-directed practise to achieve the same goal of the emergence of deeper wisdom. It is evident, even in his introduction to the topic, that he has demonstrable verbal clarity saying (MN 10, SuttaCentral, 2020, paras. 3–4):

> *"Mendicants, the four kinds of mindfulness meditation are the path to convergence. They are in order to purify sentient beings, to get past sorrow and crying, to make an end of pain and sadness, to end the cycle of suffering, and to realize extinguishment."*
>
> *"What four? It's when a mendicant meditates by observing an aspect of the body—keen, aware, and mindful, rid of desire and aversion for the world. They meditate observing an aspect of feelings—keen, aware, and mindful, rid of desire and aversion for the world. They meditate observing an aspect of the mind—keen, aware, and mindful, rid of desire and aversion for the world. They meditate observing an aspect of principles—keen, aware, and mindful, rid of desire and aversion for the world."*

The rest of this teaching breaks the topic down into four aspects with clear instruction for each contemplation, developing mindfulness and deepening wisdom. It is important to note that contemporary education has rediscovered mindfulness as something of value to develop with teachers being able to take courses for themselves and their students. Mindfulness training has been a key part of the education given orally by monks and nuns in temples and meditation classes developed from the fully explicated teaching given by the Buddha in the *Mahāsatipaṭṭhānasutta* (MN 22, SuttaCentral, 2020). Variations and adaptation of mindfulness teachings are now available in apps on mobile phones. Even so, a signature element of mindfulness teaching is the verbal clarity of instruction that remains essential, something developed by the Buddha all those years ago.

5.2.2 Teaching for Understanding

The second aspect to note of the Buddha's teaching approach to helping students in *Pariyatti* learning the doctrine was that he explicitly taught in such a way that his students might develop inner wisdom. Thus, he taught to develop their understanding of this important topic. As such, he spent 45 years developing topics that were associated with his key ideas found in the *cattari ariya saccani* Four Noble Truths and the *aṭṭhaṅgikaṃ maggaṃ* Noble Eightfold Path. These are ideas that are complex and his students regarded them of being worthy of learning, interesting and relevant to their lives and their pursuit of the development of inner wisdom. He offered learners many strategies by which to investigate, encouraged them to practice his methods and come to their own conclusions based on these experiences and their arising understanding. Contemporary teachers would recognise these as being key elements in engaging a student and teaching for understanding (Killen, 2013, pp. 47–55). As Killen notes, the combination of teaching for understanding with constructivist approaches to student learning combine to form a powerful teaching and learning synergy. The Buddha exemplified this approach, appealing to students at different stages of development and levels of understanding, providing a variety of strategies and activities, as the *Aṭṭhasatasutta* (SN 36.22, SuttaCentral, 2020) demonstrates. Students often asked him why he gave different teachings at different times about the same topic and he gave this explanation of the differentiation he used to explain the same topic (SN 36.22, SuttaCentral, 2020, paras. 1–10), saying:

> *"Mendicants, I will teach you an exposition of the teaching on the hundred and eight. Listen …*
>
> *And what is the exposition of the teaching on the hundred and eight? Mendicants, in one explanation I've spoken of two feelings. In another explanation I've spoken of three feelings, or five, six, eighteen, thirty-six, or a hundred and eight feelings.*
>
> *And what are the two feelings? Physical and mental. These are called the two feelings.*
>
> *And what are the three feelings? Pleasant, painful, and neutral feelings. …*
>
> *And what are the five feelings? The faculties of pleasure, pain, happiness, sadness, and equanimity. …*
>
> *And what are the six feelings? Feeling born of eye contact … ear contact … nose contact … tongue contact … body contact … mind contact. …*
>
> *And what are the eighteen feelings? There are six preoccupations with happiness, six preoccupations with sadness, and six preoccupations with equanimity. …*
>
> *And what are the thirty-six feelings? Six kinds of lay happiness and six kinds of renunciate happiness. Six kinds of lay sadness and six kinds of renunciate sadness. Six kinds of lay equanimity and six kinds of renunciate equanimity. …*
>
> *And what are the hundred and eight feelings? Thirty-six feelings in the past, future, and present. These are called the hundred and eight feelings.*
> *This is the exposition of the teaching on the hundred and eight."*

He also gives an extended teaching about the need to teach for student understanding in the *Khettūpamasutta* (SN 42.7, SuttaCentral, 2020, paras. 1–14), saying:

> *At one time the Buddha was staying near Nālandā in Pāvārika's mango grove. Then Asibandhaka's son the chief went up to the Buddha, bowed, sat down to one side, and said to him:*
>
> *"Sir, doesn't the Buddha live full of compassion for all living beings?"*
>
> *"Yes, chief."*
>
> *"Well, sir, why exactly do you teach some people thoroughly and others less thoroughly?"*
>
> *"Well then, chief, I'll ask you about this in return, and you can answer as you like. What do you think? Suppose a farmer has three fields: one's good, one's average, and one's poor—bad ground of sand and salt. What do you think? When that farmer wants to plant seeds, where would he plant them first: the good field, the average one, or the poor one?"*
>
> *"Sir, he'd plant them first in the good field, then the average, then he may or may not plant seed in the poor field. Why is that? Because at least it can be fodder for the cattle."*

"To me, the monks and nuns are like the good field. I teach them the Dhamma that's good in the beginning, good in the middle, and good in the end, meaningful and well-phrased. And I reveal a spiritual practice that's entirely full and pure. Why is that? Because they live with me as their island, protection, shelter, and refuge."

To me, the laymen and laywomen are like the average field. I also teach them the Dhamma that's good in the beginning, good in the middle, and good in the end, meaningful and well-phrased. And I reveal a spiritual practice that's entirely full and pure. Why is that? Because they live with me as their island, protection, shelter, and refuge."

To me, the ascetics, brahmins, and wanderers who follow other paths are like the poor field, the bad ground of sand and salt. I also teach them the Dhamma that's good in the beginning, good in the middle, and good in the end, meaningful and well-phrased. And I reveal a spiritual practice that's entirely full and pure. Why is that? Hopefully they might understand even a single sentence, which would be for their lasting welfare and happiness."

5.2.3 Teacher Pedagogical Techniques for Pariyatti *Stage*

As can be seen in the previous examples, the Buddha employed a number of pedagogical techniques to convey his explicit instruction while teaching for student understanding. The techniques most commonly employed by him were: standardisation of words and phrases, repetition, the use of numbers, mnemonics, the use of familiar, local languages, using figurative languages, such as metaphor, simile, and analogy. Sujato and Brahmali (2015, p. 77) point to the highly distinctive style of the Buddha observing that:

This can be seen in a number of aspects of the EBTs such as the large number of similes, analogies and metaphors that are vivid, precise in application, realistic and local, and formal in presentation; the analytical approach to language, which was unknown before the Buddha; use of irony and humour; and internal consistency and coherence ... This distinctive personal style is quite different from anything found in other Buddhist literature, or even in the Upaniṣads.

As was discussed in previous chapters, over 45 years the Buddha refined his teachings by the teacherly process of daily repetition and discussion through a question and answer format with his students, followers, and the wider community. In examining the EBTs, I found evidence that he was taking words and concepts that would have been familiar to his audience, such as a simple idea about reincarnation turning the concept onto a much more complex understanding of *Paṭiccasamuppādasutta* (SN 12.1, SuttaCentral, 2020) dependent origination. Over the span of years, the *Suttas* reflect the standardisation of this teaching, sometimes given in full and sometimes through a particular aspect, where the standardisation of the language and his meanings for the words and phrases he used contributed to his approach of explicit instruction and also supported his teaching for understanding. This process of standardisation and repetition in familiar local language has contributed significantly to the ability of his teachings to have been preserved into the present era as well as being of great support to those who were learning this path to wisdom from him.

Another notable pedagogical technique was the Buddha's use of numbers and other mnemonics to aid learners in the memorisation of his teachings. One of the five books of the Sutta Nikāya is the Aṅguttara Nikāya is an extensive collection of the Buddha's teachings ordered by number. Other *Suttas* also use numbering to aid memorisation. For example, in the *Okkanta*, the Buddha teaches ten doctrinal items and presents it according to a set pattern. In a teaching known as the *Cakkhu Vagga* (SN 25.1-10, SuttaCentral, 2020) the Buddha employs standardisation of words and phrases, in a pattern supported by a specific number of key elements as a way of teaching ten items of importance to his core ideas, aiding memory and showing their interrelatedness. For example, in the *Cakkhusutta* teaching about the eye (SN 25.1, SuttaCentral, 2020, para. 1)[1] it is explained that:

> *"One with faith in the teachings on the six interior sense fields is called a 'follower by faith', while someone with conceptual understanding is called a 'follower of the teachings'. But someone who sees them directly is called a stream-enterer."*

In the *Samphassajasutta* teaching about feelings (SN 25.5, SuttaCentral, 2020, para. 1)[2] the Buddha explains that:

> *"One with faith in the teachings on the six kinds of feeling is called a 'follower by faith', while someone with conceptual understanding is called a 'follower of the teachings'. But someone who sees them directly is called a stream-enterer."*

In the *Pathavīdhātusutta* teaching about the elements (SN 25.9, SuttaCentral, 2020, para. 1)[3] the Buddha explains that:

> *"One with faith in the teachings on the four physical elements is called a 'follower by faith', while someone with conceptual understanding is called a 'follower of the teachings'. But someone who sees them directly is called a stream-enterer."*

In these short, simple examples, one can gain a sense of the way these techniques of mnemonics and numbering were used. These were skills of oratory and exposition that were commonly employed by the Buddha to meet the needs of an audience that were listening and trying to remember his teachings. Without the support of written down teachings, or even the extensive digital repositories available in the present era, these techniques were a vital element in the preservation of his discourses.

Possibly most remarkable, within these teachings, was the Buddha's ability to choose vivid and suitable figurative language and analogies that remain a signature of his long teaching career. While being explicit in the assemblage of his teachings, he employed figurative language to support his listeners in developing and deepening their understanding. Sujato and Brahmali (2015) and Gombrich (2013) note his use of simile and metaphor, for example, in general terms. Hecker's (2009) in-depth examination of the similes the Buddha used provides a rich canvass of evocative imagery of relevance to his listeners. Here, I want to emphasise the Buddha's use of

---

[1] See the expanded description on the top right corner under *Cakkhusutta* (https://suttacentral.net/sn25.1/en/sujato).

[2] See the expanded description on the top right corner under *Samphassajasutta* (https://suttacentral.net/sn25.5/en/sujato).

[3] See the expanded description on the top right corner under *Pathavīdhātusutta* (https://suttacentral.net/sn25.9/en/sujato).

analogy and figurative language as pedagogical techniques, where he often gave an imaginative meaning to his explanation while also creating special oratorical, emotive effect. I am differentiating his use of simile, as being a figure of speech that compares two separate concepts through the use of a clear connecting word such as 'like', 'as', or 'in the same way', with metaphor, where he simply posits that two separate things are the same in terms of the characteristic to which he draws attention. For example, in the *Opamma Saṃyutta* (SN 20, SuttaCentral, 2020) Linked Discourses with Similes, there are twelve teachings where the Buddha employs similes to illustrate diverse points of the teaching. In the *Kūṭasutta* (SN 20.1, SuttaCentral, 2020, paras. 1–4) the Buddha uses the simile of a roof peak to describe how demolishing the roof peak is like demolishing ignorance through practice, saying:

> *So, I have heard. At one time the Buddha was staying near Sāvatthī in Jeta's Grove, Anāthapiṇḍika's monastery.*
>
> *There the Buddha ... said:*
>
> *"Mendicants, the rafters of a bungalow all lean to the peak and meet at the peak, and when the peak is demolished they're all demolished too. In the same way any unskilful qualities are rooted in ignorance and meet in ignorance, and when ignorance is demolished they're all demolished too."*
>
> *"So, you should train like this: 'We will stay diligent.' That's how you should train."*

There are eleven similar examples using familiar objects and circumstances, such as a fingernail, families, a spear, the archers, the drum peg, wood blocks, a bull elephant, a cat, and a jackal in this set of teachings that the Buddha employs to highlight certain points on a topic such as sensual pleasure, something that he was asked about on numerous occasions and in many different places. For example, in the *Alagaddūpamasutta* (MN 22, SuttaCentral, 2020, para. 11) the Buddha reminds Ariṭṭha, formerly of the vulture killers, of the many similes used to explain his teaching on sensual pleasure saying:

> *"... With the simile of the skeleton...with the simile of the piece of meat...with the simile of the grass torch...with the simile of the pit of coals...with the simile of the dream...with the simile of the borrowed goods...with the simile of fruits on a tree...with the simile of the butcher's knife and block...with the simile of the sword stake...with the simile of the snake's head, I have stated that sensual pleasures provide little gratification, much suffering and despair, and that the danger in them is still more."*

Across the *Suttas*, one can find many such examples of simile and metaphor where the Buddha aims to teach for understanding. He also employs analogy to do some of this work. He sometimes uses similes and metaphors to make an analogy but, in his analogies, he also provides an additional explanation to highlight his main point. Following the above explanation, the Buddha goes on to explain to his *Sangha* a deeper explanation of his use of simile by using another simile of the *kullaṃ* raft, so he can give a fuller, analogous explanation (MN 22, SuttaCentral, 2020, paras. 24–28), saying:

> *"Bhikkhus, I shall show you how the Dhamma is similar to a raft, being for the purpose of crossing over, not for the purpose of grasping. Listen and attend closely to what I shall say."*

> *"Yes, venerable sir," the bhikkhus replied. The Blessed One said this:*
>
> *"Bhikkhus, suppose a man in the course of a journey saw a great expanse of water, whose near shore was dangerous and fearful and whose further shore was safe and free from fear, but there was no ferryboat or bridge for going to the far shore. Then he thought: 'There is this great expanse of water, whose near shore is dangerous and fearful and whose further shore is safe and free from fear, but there is no ferryboat or bridge for going to the far shore. Suppose I collect grass, twigs, branches, and leaves and bind them together into a raft, and supported by the raft and, making an effort with my hands and feet, I got safely across to the far shore.' And then the man collected grass, twigs, branches, and leaves and bound them together into a raft, and supported by the raft and making an effort with his hands and feet, he got safely across to the far shore. Then, when he had got across and had arrived at the far shore, he might think thus: 'This raft has been very helpful to me, since supported by it and, making an effort with my hands and feet, I got safely across to the far shore. Suppose I were to hoist it on my head or load it on my shoulder, and then go wherever I want.' Now, bhikkhus, what do you think? By doing so, would that man be doing what should be done with that raft?"*
>
> *"No, venerable sir."*
>
> *"By doing what would that man be doing what should be done with that raft? Here, bhikkhus, when that man got across and had arrived at the far shore, he might think thus: 'This raft has been very helpful to me, since supported by it and making an effort with my hands and feet, I got safely across to the far shore. Suppose I were to haul it onto the dry land or set it adrift in the water, and then go wherever I want.' Now, bhikkhus, it is by so doing that that man would be doing what should be done with that raft. So, I have shown you how the Dhamma is similar to a raft, being for the purpose of crossing over, not for the purpose of grasping."*
>
> *"Bhikkhus, when you know the Dhamma to be similar to a raft, you should abandon even the teachings, how much more so things contrary to the teachings."*

In the *Uttiyasutta* (AN 10.95, SuttaCentral, 2020, paras. 12–14) Ananda, one of the monks who became most influential in assembling and codifying the Buddha's teachings, mentions his conscious use of an analogy to explain a point to Uttiya, saying:

> *"... I will give you an analogy, for there are cases where it is through the use of analogy that intelligent people can understand the meaning of what is being said."*
>
> *"Uttiya, suppose that there was a royal frontier fortress with strong ramparts, strong walls & arches, and a single gate. In it would be a wise, competent, & knowledgeable gatekeeper to keep out those he didn't know and to let in those he did. Patrolling the path around the city, he wouldn't see a crack or an opening in the walls big enough for even a cat to slip through. Although he wouldn't know that 'So-and-so many creatures enter or leave the city,' he would know this: 'Whatever large creatures enter or leave the city all enter or leave it through this gate.'"*
>
> *"In the same way, the Tathagata isn't concerned with whether all the cosmos or half of it or a third of it will be led to release by means of that [Dhamma]. But he does know this: 'All those who have been led, are being led, or will be led [to release] from the cosmos have done so, are doing so, or will do so after having abandoned the five hindrances—those defilements of awareness that weaken discernment—having well-established their minds in the four frames of reference, and having developed, as they have come to be, the seven factors for Awakening."*

5.2.4 Learner Engagement Practices for Pariyatti *Stage*

As teachers know, in an ideally synergistic process, the teacher's approaches and techniques are met with certain engagement practices that together create understanding. There are three aspects of note in the *Suttas* that I will highlight in this examination of the first stage of *Pariyatti* learning the doctrine: co-operative learning through memorisation and group recital.

In the *Satiuppajjanapañha* (Mil 3.7.1, SuttaCentral, 2020), King Milinda asks a question of Nāgasena about memory. Nāgasena was a famous teacher of the *Buddha-Dhamma* after the passing of the Buddha. Nāgasena's answer provides some insight into how memory was understood as being caused by sixteen different stimuli. In this explanation, it is also possible to see the ongoing use of numerical ordering, analogy, metaphor, and simile to support Nāgasena being able to give an explicit teaching, sixteen stimuli, while teaching for understanding through the use of figurative language that would have been familiar to King Milinda who asked (Mil 3.7.1, SuttaCentral, 2020, paras. 1–3):

> *The king said: 'In how many ways, Nāgasena, does memory spring up?'*
>
> *'In sixteen ways, O king. That is to say: by personal experience, as when the venerable Ānanda, or the devoted woman Khujjuttarā, or any others who had that power, called to mind their previous births—or by outward aid, as when others continue to remind one who is by nature forgetful—or by the impression made by the greatness of some occasion, as kings remember their coronation day, or as we remember the day of our conversion-by the impression made by joy, as when one remembers that which gave him pleasure—or by the impression made by sorrow, as when one remembers that which pained him—or from similarity of appearance, as on seeing one like them we call to mind the mother or father or sister or brother, or on seeing a camel or an ox or an ass we call to mind others like them—or by difference of appearance, as when we remember that such and such a colour, sound, smell, taste, or touch belong to such and such a thing—or by the knowledge of speech, as when one who is by nature forgetful is reminded by others and then himself remembers—or by a sign, as when we recognise a draught bullock by a brand mark or some other sign-or from effort to recollect as when one by nature forgetful is made to recollect by being urged again and again: "try and think of it"—or by calculation, as when one knows by the training he has received in writing that such and such a letter ought to follow after such and such a one—or by arithmetic, as when accountants do big sums by their knowledge of figures—or by learning by heart, as the repeaters of the scriptures by their skill in learning by heart recollect so much—or by meditation, as when a Bhikkhu calls to mind his temporary states in days gone by—by reference to a book, as when kings calling to mind a previous regulation, say: "Bring the book here," and remind themselves out of that—or by a pledge, as when at the sight of goods deposited a man recollects (the circumstances under which they were pledged)—or by association, as when one remembers a thing because one has seen it, or a sound because one has heard it, or an odour because one has smelt it, or a touch because one has felt it, or a concept because one has perceived it.'*
>
> *'Very good, Nāgasena!'*

The practice of co-operative learning through memorisation and group recital began while the Buddha was still alive. In the oral world, the followers of the Buddha's teachings began to assemble his teachings, discuss them, and commit them to memory. This involved ongoing discussions among themselves and also with the Buddha when he returned to their town or village over his years of teaching across the region (see Chap. 2, this edition for more detail). They discussed various points of understanding they had, arising from the Buddha's teachings and also from their experiences, checking for meaning and drawing on other teachings and discussions to establish what was to be memorised. To achieve their goal of protecting, maintaining, and preserving the Buddha's teachings, the *Sangha* of monks and nuns and his lay followers began the practice of group recital. This practice continues to be the principle way of transmission in Buddhist temples across Asia, where it is still possible to hear monks and nuns chanting *Suttas* over many hours. These feats of memorisation through group recital are remarkable in a time when so much human knowledge is being committed to written and digital forms that are far more transient in their capacity to be forgotten. The oral method of chanting has endured because it relies only on human motivation in order to provide a tangible, cooperative learning environment for those who believe that these teachings are worthy of preservation and unbroken transmission to future generations. It does not rely on the written word and its digital counterparts where books can disappear and digital platforms become corrupted or unreadable. The vulnerability of the oral methods of cooperative learning is that the transmission relies on the reliability of the memory of the teacher and other chanters. This is the vulnerability that has caused aspects of the teaching to take on the personal understandings and experiences of the teacher. Killen (2013) provides a succinct explanation of the benefits and drawback of cooperative learning that have echoes of the descriptions of cooperative learning found across the EBTs. Killen (2013, pp. 227–228) emphasises the aspect of positive interdependence whereby those involved need to form a cohesive group to achieve specific learning goals and have ongoing direct interaction over time. The temple environment provided the ideal context to support cooperative learning in ways that would be recognised by the contemporary teacher (Pichard & Lagirarde, 2003). The *Sangha* and lay followers of the Buddha had the interpersonal skills and ability to reflect on what they had learned, to work cooperatively in a manner that has ensured that, over 2,500 years the words of the Buddha, his teachings, and his manner of teaching have been preserved. To achieve such a remarkable accomplishment, those learning from the Buddha also needed to involve themselves in the second stage of the *Majjhima Patipada* Middle Way using the techniques for *paṭipatti* 'practising it [the *Buddha-Dhamma*]'.

5.3 Stage 2: *Paṭipatti* Practising the Doctrine

It is important to highlight that despite the importance of the context of cooperative learning that has carried the *Buddha-Dhamma* into the present day, it has been the autonomous efforts of myriad humans who have been individually motivated to seek out and practice the Buddha's teachings. While the Buddha's pedagogical approach in Stage 1 was shaped by explicit methods, he taught for understanding. In doing so, he urged those who listened to him to test everything they heard, to believe nothing, and to effectively construct their own meaning of their experiences. He was confident

Table 5.2 Teaching strategies and techniques for *Paṭipatti* practising the doctrine

Teaching strategies	Teacher pedagogical techniques	Learner engagement practices
Experiential learning Constructivist practices	Encouraging students to practice Modelling good practice Providing clear instruction for practice Tailoring practices to the needs and abilities of the individual learner	Believe nothing Take a gradual path Follow the *Paññanaya* wisdom method • *Sīla* moral conduct practices • *Samādhi* Calm meditation practices • *Vipassanā* Clear-seeing insight practices

that through hearing his explanations, that with experience, his followers would have the same experiences and come to the same insights about the development of their wisdom as he had done and found. The Buddha modelled his teaching but expected his students to take opportunity to experience is methods for themselves. His teachings invited his students to change their mental and emotional maps about how they perceived their world. He taught and modelled axiological (values), ontological, and epistemological aspects. He provided his students with many opportunities to examine *sīla* their moral and ethical behaviour (Table 5.2).

These examinations led to being able to go inward, supported by *samādhi* calm meditation practices that would lead to single-pointed concentration. He encouraged his students to engage in *vipassanā* epistemological reflection practices that would allow discernment to arise. This stage of the *Majjhima Patipada* Middle Way relied on education theories that would employ experiential learning and be called constructivist approaches to teaching and learning (Killen, 2013, pp. 41–47). This second stage of *Paṭipatti* is most closely aligned to Bloom's 'Apply' category of cognitive development (Krathwohl et al., 2001) involving cognitive processes of executing and implementing.

5.3.1 Teacher Pedagogical Techniques for **Paṭipatti** *Stage*

There are four techniques that I have identified as being key to understanding how the Buddha taught students to practice his teachings: encouraging students to practice, modelling practice, providing clear instruction for practice, and tailoring practices to the needs and abilities of the individual learner. These four techniques were the anchors for opportunities for experience-derived understanding to arise.

5.3.1.1 Encouraging Learners to Practice

In the *Sikkhāpadasutta* (AN 4.99, SuttaCentral, 2020, paras. 1, 5), the Buddha identifies one of four types of students as being an ideal for encouraging others to practice, here explaining through the lens of *Sīla* moral conduct practices that:

> *"Monks, these four types of individuals are to be found existing in the world. Which four? The one who practices for his own benefit but not for that of others. The one who practices for the benefit of others but not for his own. The one who practices neither for his own benefit nor for that of others. The one who practices for his own benefit and for that of others."*
>
> ...
>
> *"And how is one an individual who practices for his own benefit and for that of others? There is the case where a certain individual himself abstains from the taking of life and encourages others in undertaking abstinence from the taking of life. He himself abstains from stealing and encourages others in undertaking abstinence from stealing. He himself abstains from sexual misconduct and encourages others in undertaking abstinence from sexual misconduct. He himself abstains from lying and encourages others in undertaking abstinence from lying. He himself abstains from intoxicants that cause heedlessness and encourages others in undertaking abstinence from intoxicants that cause heedlessness. Such is the individual who practices for his own benefit and for that of others."*

5.3.1.2 Modelling Good Practice

The Buddha also emphasised the need for teachers of the *Buddha-Dhamma* to model good practices such as in the *Alaṃsutta* (AN 8.62, SuttaCentral, 2020, para. 1) where he describes the six qualities of someone who wants to teach, saying:

> *"Mendicants, a mendicant with six qualities is good enough for themselves and others. What six? A mendicant is quick-witted when it comes to skilful teachings. They readily memorize the teachings they've heard. They examine the meaning of teachings they've memorized. Understanding the meaning and the teaching, they practice accordingly. They're a good speaker. Their voice is polished, clear, articulate, and expresses the meaning. They educate, encourage, fire up, and inspire their spiritual companions. A mendicant with these six qualities is good enough for themselves and others."*

5.3.1.3 Providing Clear Instruction for Practice

The Buddha also highlighted the need for a teacher to provide clear instructions for practice. This point is also reinforced in the other 2 stages but is of particular pedagogical importance here because, without clear guidance, also known as explicit instruction, the embedded principle of the constructivist approach would founder. In the *Sālasutta* (SN 47.4, SuttaCentral, 2020, paras. 1–3) the Buddha is instructing some *bhikkhus* monks about how to achieve and maintain a calm meditation state using *ekaggacittā* single-pointed awareness practices:

On one occasion the Blessed One was dwelling among the Kosalans at the brahmin village of Sala. There the Blessed One addressed the bhikkhus thus:

"Bhikkhus, those bhikkhus who are newly ordained, not long gone forth, recently come to this Dhamma and Discipline, should be exhorted, settled, and established by you in the development of the four establishments of mindfulness. What four?"

"Come, friends, dwell contemplating the body in the body, ardent, clearly comprehending, unified, with limpid mind, concentrated, with one-pointed mind, in order to know the body as it really is. Dwell contemplating feelings in feelings ... in order to know feelings as they really are. Dwell contemplating mind in mind ... in order to know mind as it really is. Dwell contemplating phenomena in phenomena ... in order to know phenomena as they really are."

5.3.1.4 Tailoring Practices to the Needs and Abilities of the Individual Learner

In this teaching, he also explains about the importance of tailoring practices to the needs and abilities of the individual learner, noting the different needs of students who are at different stages of development in their practice. In the *Vitthārasutta* (AN 4.162, SuttaCentral, 2020, paras. 1–6), he provides precise detail for four different modes of practice that should be chosen depending on the characteristics of the learner, saying:

"Monks, there are these four modes of practice. Which four? Painful practice with slow intuition, painful practice with quick intuition, pleasant practice with slow intuition, & pleasant practice with quick intuition."

"And which is painful practice with slow intuition? There is the case where a certain individual is normally of an intensely passionate nature. He perpetually experiences pain & distress born of passion. Or he is normally of an intensely aversive nature. He perpetually experiences pain & distress born of aversion. Or he is normally of an intensely deluded nature. He perpetually experiences pain & distress born of delusion. These five faculties of his—the faculty of conviction, the faculty of persistence, the faculty of mindfulness, the faculty of concentration, the faculty of discernment—appear weakly. Because of their weakness, he attains only slowly the immediacy that leads to the ending of the effluents. This is called painful practice with slow intuition."

"And which is painful practice with quick intuition? There is the case where a certain individual is normally of an intensely passionate nature. He perpetually experiences pain & distress born of passion. Or he is normally of an intensely aversive nature. He perpetually experiences pain & distress born of aversion. Or he is normally of an intensely deluded nature. He perpetually experiences pain & distress born of delusion. These five faculties of his—the faculty of conviction, the faculty of persistence, the faculty of mindfulness, the faculty of concentration, the faculty of discernment—appear intensely. Because of their intensity, he attains quickly the immediacy that leads to the ending of the effluents. This is called painful practice with quick intuition."

"And which is pleasant practice with slow intuition? There is the case where a certain individual is normally not of an intensely passionate nature. He does not perpetually experience pain & distress born of passion. Or he is normally not of an intensely aversive nature. He does not perpetually experience pain & distress born of aversion. Or he is normally not of an intensely deluded nature. He does not perpetually experience pain & distress born of delusion. These five faculties of his—the faculty of conviction, the faculty of persistence,

the faculty of mindfulness, the faculty of concentration, the faculty of discernment—appear weakly. Because of their weakness, he attains only slowly the immediacy that leads to the ending of the effluents. This is called pleasant practice with slow intuition."

"And which is pleasant practice with quick intuition? There is the case where a certain individual is normally not of an intensely passionate nature. He does not perpetually experience pain & distress born of passion. Or he is normally not of an intensely aversive nature. He does not perpetually experience pain & distress born of aversion. Or he is normally not of an intensely deluded nature. He does not perpetually experience pain & distress born of delusion. These five faculties of his—the faculty of conviction, the faculty of persistence, the faculty of mindfulness, the faculty of concentration, the faculty of discernment—appear intensely. Because of their intensity, he attains quickly the immediacy that leads to the ending of the effluents. This is called pleasant practice with quick intuition."

"These are the four modes of practice."

These explanations are maintained to this day, discussed by teachers of the Dhamma with those they are training to teach. Such training involves learning how to identify the needs of each student and relies on oral transmission as it has done for 2,500 years. The exhortations to practice continue to be very strong within temples and on course about Buddhism and these pedagogical techniques are used.

5.3.2 Learner Engagement Practices for **Paṭipatti** *Stage*

There are three learner engagement practices that I have identified that the Buddha regularly referred to in discussing his teachings and how to practice them. He encouraged his students to believe nothing he taught without confirming for themselves by their experiences that what he was teaching was true. For example, in the *Kesamuttisutta* (AN 3.65, SuttaCentral, 2020, paras. 1, 19), it is recorded that:

On one occasion the Blessed One was wandering on tour among the Kosalans together with a large Saṅgha of monks when he reached the town of the Kālāmas named Kesaputta ... "Come, Kālāmas, do not go by oral tradition, by lineage of teaching, by hearsay, by a collection of scriptures, by logical reasoning, by inferential reasoning, by reasoned cogitation, by the acceptance of a view after pondering it, by the seeming competence of a speaker, or because you think: 'The ascetic is our guru.' But when you know for yourselves: 'These things are wholesome; these things are blameless; these things are praised by the wise; these things, if accepted and undertaken, lead to welfare and happiness,' then you should live in accordance with them."

He emphasised that this was a gradual path of developing wisdom through a process of following his *Buddha-Dhamma* core curriculum of the *cattari ariya saccani* Four Noble Truths and the *aṭṭhaṅgikaṃ maggaṃ* Noble Eightfold Path (see Appendix C). To follow this path, he developed guidance for his students about following the *Paññanaya* wisdom method. This involved them doing *sīla* moral conduct practices, *samādhi* calm meditation practices, and v*ipassanā* clear-seeing insight practices that provided them with the necessary experience-derived, tacit understanding of the teachings such that they could confidently move to the third stage of the *Majjhima Patipada* Middle Way method developed by the Buddha.

5.4 Stage 3: *Paṭivedha* Understanding the Experience

In this third stage of the method, the first round of the Buddha's approach comes together. In the *Paṭivedha* stage, the teacher helps the student to understand their experiences, also referred to as 'penetrating the doctrine', guiding them to a deeper understanding of what had been taught in Stage 1 (Table 5.3).

Part of the teacher's role in this stage is to assess learner readiness to move into more complex teaching of the core curriculum, thereby returning to Stage 1 to begin the process again, as was noted earlier, imagined as a spiral of development. This third stage of *Paṭivedha* is most closely aligned to Bloom's 'Analyze' and 'Evaluate' categories of cognitive development (Krathwohl et al., 2001) involving cognitive processes of differentiating, organising, attributing, checking, and critiquing.

In this third stage, the Buddha combines the experiences of the student with questioning and encouragement to reflect helps the student to make sense of their experiences. Such questioning and reflection are interweaved with teaching for understanding in such discussions to enable constructivist elements to emerge. The Buddha assists his students to reflect and change their cognitive and affective maps in the gradual manner of his approach to support their development in wisdom. This approach is neatly summarised in the *Paṭisaṅkhānabalasutta* (AN 4.155, SuttaCentral, 2020, para. 1) Power of Reflection Sutta where he affirms that:

> *"Mendicants, there are these four powers. What four? The powers of reflection, development, blamelessness, and inclusiveness. These are the four powers."*

5.4.1 *Teacher Pedagogical Techniques for* Paṭivedha *Stage*

To support the development of these powers, the teacher is encouraged to use a question and answer format. While this might involve some explicit teaching, in this third stage, the questions and answers are more of a dialogue with the student to probe their experiences and help them to penetrate the deeper meaning of them. The Buddha's technique is mainly to use student reflections on their experiences

Table 5.3 Teaching strategies and techniques for *Paṭivedha* understanding of experiences

Teaching strategies	Teacher pedagogical practices	Learner engagement practices
Combining constructivist approach with teaching for understanding: • Questioning • Encouragement to reflect	Q & A Using student reflections on experience and questions: acknowledging, modifying, applying, comparing, and summarising	Reflecting and analysing • Inquiry • Problem solving

and, depending on the question, experience, or context, acknowledging, modifying, applying, comparing, and summarising to aid the development of *Paṭivedha.*

5.4.1.1 Question and Answer

In Stage 1, when I was discussing *Pariyatti* learning the doctrine, I gave the example in the *Alagaddūpamasutta* (MN 22, SuttaCentral, 2020) of the Buddha using similes to explain to Ariṭṭha, formerly of the vulture killers, the dangers of sensual pleasure. After he concludes his discussion with Ariṭṭha, he then uses this teaching to instruct the *Sangha* about the need to undertake this third stage, explaining in the Simile of the Snake (MN 22, SuttaCentral, 2020, paras. 19–20, 23), that:

> *"Here, bhikkhus, some misguided men learn the Dhamma—discourses, stanzas, expositions, verses, exclamations, sayings, birth stories, marvels, and answers to questions—but having learned the Dhamma, they do not examine the meaning of those teachings with wisdom. Not examining the meaning of those teachings with wisdom, they do not gain a reflective acceptance of them. Instead they learn the Dhamma only for the sake of criticising others and for winning in debates, and they do not experience the good for the sake of which they learned the Dhamma. Those teachings, being wrongly grasped by them, conduce to their harm and suffering for a long time. Why is that? Because of the wrong grasp of those teachings."*
>
> *"Suppose a man needing a snake, seeking a snake, wandering in search of a snake, saw a large snake and grasped its coils or its tail. It would turn back on him and bite his hand or his arm or one of his limbs, and because of that he would come to death or deadly suffering. Why is that? Because of his wrong grasp of the snake. So too, here some misguided men learn the Dhamma...Why is that? Because of the wrong grasp of those teachings ..."*
>
> *"Therefore, bhikkhus, when you understand the meaning of my statements, remember it accordingly; and when you do not understand the meaning of my statements, then ask either me about it or those bhikkhus who are wise."*

There are numerous examples of the Buddha and the teachers who followed him and used his methods acknowledging, modifying, applying, comparing, and summarising experiences of their students to help them to understand and develop.

5.4.2 *Learner Engagement Practices for* Paṭivedha *Stage*

The student is asked to undertake three practices in this third stage: reflecting and analysing, problem-solving, and ongoing inquiry. It is recorded in the *Dhammānudhammapaṭipannasutta* (Iti 86, SuttaCentral, 2020, paras. 3–4) that the culmination of these allows for the development of inner wisdom, with well-developed abilities to remain aware and restrained in mind and conduct, will achieve inner peace:

> *A bhikkhu enjoying the Dhamma*
> *And delighting in the Dhamma,*
> *Reflecting upon the Dhamma,*

Does not fall from the true Dhamma.
Whether walking or standing,
Sitting or lying down,
With mind inwardly restrained,
He attains to lasting peace.

The Buddha gave numerous teaching that used analogies and figurative language to support his students to penetrate their experiences and thoughts. In a discussion with his son, Rāhula, in the *Ambalaṭṭhikarāhulovādasutta* (MN 61, SuttaCentral, 2020, paras. 17–20) he uses a combination of acknowledgement of his son's growing understanding, with techniques of comparison and summary to help him to understand a particular point, engaging Rāhula in dialogue about the importance of reflection:

What do you think, Rāhula? What is the purpose of a mirror?"

"It's for checking your reflection, sir."

"In the same way, deeds of body, speech, and mind should be done only after repeated checking."

"When you want to act with the body, you should check on that same deed: 'Does this act with the body that I want to do lead to hurting myself, hurting others, or hurting both? Is it unskilful, with suffering as its outcome and result?' If, while checking in this way, you know: 'This act with the body that I want to do leads to hurting myself, hurting others, or hurting both. It's unskilful, with suffering as its outcome and result.' To the best of your ability, Rāhula, you should not do such a deed. But if, while checking in this way, you know: 'This act with the body that I want to do doesn't lead to hurting myself, hurting others, or hurting both. It's skilful, with happiness as its outcome and result.' Then, Rāhula, you should do such a deed."

As the student develops the capacity to reflect, they are encouraged to also use the teachings of the Buddha to inquire into and to solve other problems they face, using the same strategies they have been taught through stages one and two. This ability to use the techniques in other contexts is similar to the final level of Bloom's 'Create' category of cognitive development (Krathwohl et al., 2001, pp. 27–37) involving cognitive processes of generating, planning, and producing (see also, Killen, 2013, pp. 27–323). In this way, the complete process supports the student to become an autonomous learner.

5.5 Educating for Wisdom

In the contemporary era, 2,500 years after the Buddha became a teacher of the path to wisdom, there are many schools and universities beginning to incorporate studies about his life and the development of Buddhism as a global religion. Less common is the examination and scholarship about the Buddha's educational approach, his methods and techniques and his core curriculum. The purpose of this monograph is to stimulate and disseminate his ideas because I believe that the development of inner wisdom is a missing piece in modern schooling and university education.

There are schools such as the Daylesford Dharma School (DDS), in rural Victoria, Australia that are developing aspects of his teachings, particularly providing opportunity for students to practice aspects of the teachings, given by the teachers in age-appropriate forms.

As the first publicly-funded school in Australia to be established according to the philosophy of the Buddha, DDS is finding its way and working out what it means to be a dharma-inspired school in a country such as Australia that is experiencing the third wave of expansion of the Buddha's ideas (see Chap. 3, this edition). For example, for *sīla* moral development, all school policies are all held together by the *pañca-sila* Five Precepts, the Buddhist guiding principles for living. These are, as worded by the school as:

1. Deep Listening and Loving Speech;
2. Generosity;
3. Bodily Responsibility;
4. Mindful Consumption; and,
5. Reverence for All Life.

The teachers help the students to make these real in the classroom and the playground.

For the development of *samādhi* serenity, each school day begins with the Awareness Program and children arriving early to school are invited to sit quietly and meditate with the on-duty teacher. In the early days, this was not possible because there was not yet a cohesive school culture. In 2019, the children moved into a beautiful new school and became more familiar with the tempo of the school and its ways of doing schooling. In 2020, in the face of the impact of COVID-19, the teacher faced the challenge of maintaining the Awareness Program through the use of online video technologies, enabling students and their families to join the teacher. At the start of each day, everyone meditates together before returning to their class groups with their teachers. There might be a reading, a story, a discussion about a particular issue that has arisen, and the children are encouraged to raise and contribute to issues. The daily Awareness Program gives the teacher an anchor for reminding the children of the key Buddhist idea for the day and provides a point of critical reflection for strengthening the self-awareness of the children and the staff and creating learning spaces of self-responsible peace. For the development of *vipassanā* discernment, the older students are encouraged to do many projects associated with developing critical thinking skills bringing in Buddhist perspectives to help them develop this discipline. The governing board, its Dharma Education Sub-Committee and the school staff also doing a number of staff development projects and bringing Buddhist ideas to life in the daily practices of the school. This is made possible by the fertile soil carefully tilled twelve years ago to provide a space for the third generation of Buddhists with distinctly Australian characteristics to grow and thrive.

Examples such as DDS allow scholars to begin to examine what approaches used by the Buddha to cultivate inner wisdom are transferrable to the modern formal education system. Schools and universities tend to focus mainly on the transfer of knowledge and information and pay little attention to the cultivation of wisdom. With the increase in interest in Buddhist ideas in mainstream education, (e.g. the popularity of the ideas about *sati* mindfulness), it is timely to consider what materials derived from the *Buddha-Dhamma* Buddha's core curriculum the monk, nun, teacher educator, and teacher have used to undertake such work and what pedagogies have been used successfully over the past 2,500 years.

My research over many years suggests that there are enduring elements of Buddhist pedagogy and curriculum that have been transferrable across time and space. Common curriculum elements include use of scriptures found in the *Tipitaka* Buddhist Canon: the three baskets (Vinaya Pitaka, Sutta Pitaka, and Abhidhamma Pitaka), the same Vinaya, the *pañca-sila* Five Precepts, and all teachings have as their foundation the *cattari ariya saccani* Four Noble Truths and the *aṭṭhaṅgikaṃ maggaṃ* Noble Eightfold Path (see Appendix C).

The Buddha's pedagogical approach was remarkably consistent employing a three-stage method known as the *Majjhima Patipada* Middle Way comprising *pariyatti* 'learning the doctrine'), providing techniques for *paṭipatti* 'practicing it' [the doctrine], and helping students in *paṭivedha* the understanding of their experiences (Table 5.4).

He used, and taught others to use, explicit instruction and teaching for understanding blended with a strong commitment to constructivist engagement of the student. He modelled both cognitive and verbal clarity. He received questions from

Table 5.4 Summary of key elements of the Buddha's *Majjhima Patipada* Middle Way pedagogy

Teaching strategies	Teacher pedagogical techniques	Learner engagement practices
Stage 1: Pariyatti learning the doctrine		
Explicit Instruction • Cognitive clarity • Verbal clarity Teaching for understanding	Standardisation of words and phrases Numbers and Mnemonics Analogy and figurative language	Co-operative learning • Memorisation • Group recital
Stage 2: Paṭipatti practising the doctrine		
Experiential learning Constructivist practices	Encouraging students to practice Modelling good practice Providing clear instruction for practice Tailoring practices to the needs and abilities of the individual learner	Believe nothing Take a gradual path Follow the Paññanaya wisdom method • *Sīla* moral conduct practices • *Samādhi* Calm meditation practices • *Vipassanā* Clear-seeing insight practices
Stage 3: Paṭivedha understanding the experience		
Combining constructivist approach with teaching for understanding: • Questioning • Encouragement to reflect	Q & A Using student reflections on experience and questions: acknowledging, modifying, applying, comparing, and summarising	Reflecting and analysing Inquiry Problem solving

anyone but emphasised that he could, and would, only speak about those matters about which he had experienced and penetrated the deeper meaning. He encouraged his students to practice and reflect on what they experienced, always checking that they were developing an understanding of their inner wisdom through ideas and experiences that made sense to them. This element of constructivism overcame the tendency of students to believe what they were being told without making it their own. In this, I feel this was a unique educational insight and one that he referred to as distinguishing him from other teachers around him.

My analysis of the Early Buddhist Texts and in discussion with, and by observing, contemporary teachers of *Buddha-Dhamma* also shows that he employed a variety of pedagogical techniques to great effect. He created a language where people were able to apprehend the complexity of his teachings in a manner that was familiar to them. He standardised the meaning of words and phrases, regularly clarifying for his audience what he meant by his key terms. Given the conventions of orality and rhetorics of his era, he employed numbers and mnemonics to assist with the memorisation of his teachings. While much of his use of mnemonics does not translate into the English language, translators have attempted to provide verses of his discourses that convey some of the sense of the skilfulness of the Buddha as an orator. Some of the Buddha's oratorical skill is conveyed by his use of analogy and figurative language, providing enduring examples that can still evoke powerful imagery that connects with the listener or reader's emotions to create 'ah ha!' moments of understanding that work subliminally to shift a person's axiological (values), ontological, and epistemological understandings of their world towards the development of their inner wisdom.

For the Buddha though, it was not sufficient that someone simply heard his teachings. He insisted that his followers, and even those who disagreed with him, experiment with what he was telling them. He modelled what he considered to be good practice, he provided clear instruction for practice, and he tailored practices to the needs and abilities of the individual learner. After a person had undertaken a period of practice, and the Buddha assessed that they were ready, he would invite questions about what they were experiencing using a question and answer format to draw out reflections on their experience and questions. He employed specific techniques such as acknowledging, modifying, applying, comparing, and summarising that would be familiar to a classroom teacher who was undertaking a formative assessment of student learning in the contemporary era. In these discussions with particular students, he was often also teaching to a larger audience who were listening but may not yet have had the particular experience. In such a manner, often he was teaching across all three stages of his *Majjhima Patipada* Middle Way method: *pariyatti* where some of his audience might have been hearing his teaching for the first time; through his discussion of finer points of a technique he was also reminding others of techniques for *paṭipatti* practicing his teachings; and at the same time specifically helping a particular student or group of monks, nuns, lay followers, merchants, farmers, or kings in *paṭivedha* with an understanding of their experiences.

His educational approach also included some expectations about student engagement practices, knowing as he did that teaching for understanding relies on effective engagement by the student. People needed to know why his teachings were important to them and why they were willing to learn from him. His was an example of how a teacher develops an effective teaching-learning engagement at a time when teaching practices were quite didactic and hierarchical. He invited his listeners to engage in co-operative learning, using memorisation and group recital to support them being able to continue to learn when he was not living in their village or town. He encouraged them to believe nothing without experiencing it for themselves, encouraging and strengthening people's sense of autonomy. He gave them the tools to take a gradual path in their development but was able at the same time to explain the entire path so that they knew they were following a *kalyāṇamitta* reliable guide. He guided his monks, nuns, and lay followers to follow the *paññanaya* wisdom method of *sīla* moral conduct practices, *samādhi* calm meditation practices, and *vipassanā* clear-seeing insight practices, reflecting on and analysing through their use of inquiry and problem-solving.

I also found in my research and analysis that there are elements of the Buddha's educational approach and ideas that have undertaken a process of 'adaptive balancing' in order to find fertile soil in new geo-locations. I have found this through a close examination of how Buddhism has migrated through Asia to a country such as Australia to the first school inspired by Buddhist philosophy, Daylesford Dharma School and through interviews with monks, nuns, and lay teachers of Buddhism in a number of different temple traditions and schools in many countries in Asia and in Australia.

In the Australian example, a modern nation with a strong multicultural presence, I have found that: first, Buddhists who have migrated to Australia stay very close to the way that the Buddha's teachings are conveyed in their home country; second, there is an emerging form of the Buddha's teachings in both temples and schools that is adaptive to Australian culture. This is most clear in the analysis of the approach to pedagogy and curriculum taken by monks, depending on where they have undertaken their training.

Overall, the ancient educational philosophy and approach taken by the Buddha continues to be relevant in the modern world, and the expounded pedagogical pathway to the cultivation of wisdom is finding fertile soil in modern temples, schools, and universities, East and West. The challenge facing these institutions is to ensure that there remains a coherence in the commonalities of Buddhism even as the core teachings and pedagogical approach developed and enacted over 45 years by the Buddha adapt to local languages, schooling requirements, and interests. Education systems stand at an important juncture in re-imagining their role. I want future generations to have access to reliable teaching about this wonderful philosophy and its myriad forms of religious expression.

References

Suttas

SuttaCentral. (2020). Aṅguttara Nikāya 4.147. *Dutiyakālasutta* Times (2nd). [Bhikkhu Sujato, Trans.]. Retrieved December 31, 2020, from https://suttacentral.net/an4.147/en/sujato. Translated for SuttaCentral by Bhikkhu Sujato, 2018. Dedicated to the public domain via Creative Commons Zero (CC0). You are encouraged to copy, reproduce, adapt, alter, or otherwise make use of this translation in any way you wish. Attribution is appreciated but not legally required.

SuttaCentral. (2020). Aṅguttara Nikāya 8.12. *Sīhasutta* With Sīha. [Bhikkhu Sujato, Trans.]. Retrieved December 31, 2020, from https://suttacentral.net/an8.12/en/sujato. Translated for SuttaCentral by Bhikkhu Sujato, 2018. Dedicated to the public domain via Creative Commons Zero (CC0). You are encouraged to copy, reproduce, adapt, alter, or otherwise make use of this translation in any way you wish. Attribution is appreciated but not legally required.

SuttaCentral. (2020). Majjhima Nikāya 10. *Satipaṭṭhānasutta* Mindfulness Meditation. [Bhikkhu Sujato, Trans.]. Retrieved December 31, 2020, from https://suttacentral.net/mn10/en/sujato. Translated for SuttaCentral by Bhikkhu Sujato, 2018. Dedicated to the public domain via Creative Commons Zero (CC0). You are encouraged to copy, reproduce, adapt, alter, or otherwise make use of this translation in any way you wish. Attribution is appreciated but not legally required.

SuttaCentral. (2020). Dīgha Nikāya 22. *Mahāsatipaṭṭhānasutta* The Long Discourse about the Ways of Attending to Mindfulness. [Bhikkhu Anandajoti, Trans.]. Retrieved December 31, 2020, from https://suttacentral.net/dn22/en/anandajoti. Translation by Ānandajoti Bhikkhu, 3rd version, October 2011/2055. Used by kind permission. This translation, as well as extensive notes and commentary, is found on the translator's website, Ancient Buddhist Texts. Creative Commons Attribution-Share A like 3.0 Unported License. Prepared for SuttaCentral by Bhikkhu Sujato.

SuttaCentral. (2020). Saṃyutta Nikāya 36.22. *Aṭṭhasatasutta* The Explanation of the Hundred and Eight. [Bhikkhu Sujato, Trans.]. Retrieved December 31, 2020, from https://suttacentral.net/sn36.22/en/sujato. Translated for SuttaCentral by Bhikkhu Sujato, 2018. Dedicated to the public domain via Creative Commons Zero (CC0). You are encouraged to copy, reproduce, adapt, alter, or otherwise make use of this translation in any way you wish. Attribution is appreciated but not legally required.

SuttaCentral. (2020). Saṃyutta Nikāya 42.7. *Khettūpamasutta* The Simile of the Field. [Bhikkhu Sujato, Trans.]. Retrieved December 31, 2020, from https://suttacentral.net/sn42.7/en/sujato. Translated for SuttaCentral by Bhikkhu Sujato, 2018. Dedicated to the public domain via Creative Commons Zero (CC0). You are encouraged to copy, reproduce, adapt, alter, or oth-erwise make use of this translation in any way you wish. Attribution is appreciated but not legally required.

SuttaCentral. (2020). Saṃyutta Nikāya 12.1. *Paṭiccasamuppādasutta* Dependent Origination. [Bhikkhu Bodhi, Trans.]. Retrieved December 31, 2020, from https://suttacentral.net/sn12.1/en/bodhi. The Connected Discourses of the Buddha (Wisdom Publications, 2000). This excerpt from The Connected Discourses of the Buddha by Bhikkhu Bodhi is licensed under a Creative Commons Attribution-NonCommercial-NoDerivs 3.0 Unported License. Based on the work Connected Discourses of the Buddha at Wisdom Publications. Permissions beyond the scope of this license may be available at Wisdom Publications. Prepared for SuttaCentral by Blake Walsh.

SuttaCentral. (2020). Saṃyutta Nikāya 25.1-10. *Cakkhu Vagga*. [Bhikkhu Sujato, Trans.]. Retrieved December 31, 2020, from https://suttacentral.net/sn25. Translated for SuttaCentral by Bhikkhu Sujato, 2018. Dedicated to the public domain via Creative Commons Zero (CC0). You are encouraged to copy, reproduce, adapt, alter, or otherwise make use of this translation in any way you wish. Attribution is appreciated but not legally required.

SuttaCentral. (2020). Saṃyutta Nikāya 25.1. *Cakkhusutta*. The Eye. [Bhikkhu Sujato, Trans.]. Retrieved December 31, 2020, from https://suttacentral.net/sn25.1/en/sujato. Translated for SuttaCentral by Bhikkhu Sujato, 2018. Dedicated to the public domain via Creative Commons Zero

(CC0). You are encouraged to copy, reproduce, adapt, alter, or oth-erwise make use of this translation in any way you wish. Attribution is appreciated but not legally required.

SuttaCentral. (2020). Saṃyutta Nikāya 25.5. *Samphassajasutta* Feeling [Bhikkhu Sujato, Trans.]. Retrieved December 31, 2020, from https://suttacentral.net/sn25.5/en/sujato. Translated for SuttaCentral by Bhikkhu Sujato, 2018. Dedicated to the public domain via Creative Commons Zero (CC0). You are encouraged to copy, reproduce, adapt, alter, or oth-erwise make use of this translation in any way you wish. Attribution is appreciated but not legally required.

SuttaCentral. (2020). Saṃyutta Nikāya 25.9. *Pathavīdhātusutta* Elements. [Bhikkhu Sujato, Trans.]. Retrieved December 31, 2020, from https://suttacentral.net/sn25.9/en/sujato. Translated for SuttaCentral by Bhikkhu Sujato, 2018. Dedicated to the public domain via Creative Commons Zero (CC0). You are encouraged to copy, reproduce, adapt, alter, or oth-erwise make use of this translation in any way you wish. Attribution is appreciated but not legally required.

SuttaCentral. (2020). Saṃyutta Nikāya 20. *Opamma Saṃyutta. Opammavagga* Similes. [Bhikkhu Sujato, Trans.]. Retrieved December 31, 2020, from https://suttacentral.net/sn20. Translated for SuttaCentral by Bhikkhu Sujato, 2018. Dedicated to the public domain via Creative Commons Zero (CC0). You are encouraged to copy, reproduce, adapt, alter, or otherwise make use of this translation in any way you wish. Attribution is appreciated but not legally required.

SuttaCentral. (2020). Saṃyutta Nikāya 20.1. *Kūṭasutta* A Roof Peak. [Bhikkhu Sujato, Trans.]. Retrieved December 31, 2020, from https://suttacentral.net/sn20.1/en/sujato. Translated for SuttaCentral by Bhikkhu Sujato, 2018. Dedicated to the public domain via Creative Commons Zero (CC0). You are encouraged to copy, reproduce, adapt, alter, or oth-erwise make use of this translation in any way you wish. Attribution is appreciated but not legally required.

SuttaCentral. (2020). Majjhima Nikāya 22. *Alagaddūpamasutta* The Simile of the Snake. [Bhikkhu Bodhi, Trans.]. Retrieved December 31, 2020, from https://suttacentral.net/mn22/en/bodhi. The Middle Length Discourses of the Buddha (Wisdom Publications, 2009). This excerpt from The Middle Length Discourses of the Buddha by Bhikkhu Bodhi is licensed under a Creative Commons Attribution—Non Commercial—No Derivs 3.0 Unported License. Based on the work The Middle Length Discourses of the Buddha at Wisdom Publications. Permissions beyond the scope of this license may be available at Wisdom Publications. Prepared for SuttaCentral by Blake Walsh.

SuttaCentral. (2020). Aṅguttara Nikāya 10.95. *Uttiyasutta* To Uttiya. [Bhikkhu Thanissaro, Trans.]. Retrieved December 31, 2020, from https://suttacentral.net/an10.95/en/thanissaro. Translated from the Pāḷi by Thanissaro Bhikkhu. The text of this page is licensed under a Creative Commons Attribution—Non Commercial 4.0 International License. To view a copy of the license, visit http://creativecommons.org/licenses/by-nc/4.0/. Documents linked from this page may be subject to other restrictions. Transcribed from a file provided by the translator. Access to Insight (Legacy Edition), 31 November 2013, http://www.accesstoinsight.org/.

SuttaCentral. (2020). Milindapañha 3.7.1. *Satiuppajjanapañha* Causes of memory. [T. W. R. Davids, Trans.]. Retrieved December 31, 2020, from https://suttacentral.net/mil3.7.1/pli/ms. Translated from the Pāḷi by T.W. Rhys Davids. Part 1 (to section 5.4.10) was originally published as Volume xxxv of "The Sacred Books of the East", Oxford, The Clarendon Press, 1890. Part 2 (from section 5.5.1) was originally published as Volume xxxvi of "The Sacred Books of the East", Oxford, The Clarendon Press, 1894. This SuttaCentral edition was prepared by Bhikkhu Sujato based on the digital text of the Internet Sacred Text Archive. The work of the Sacred Text Archive to make this text publically available is gratefully acknowledged. In preparing this edition minor editorial changes have been made. The structure has been adapted to agree with the Mahāsaṅgīti Pāḷi text as found on SuttaCentral. In addition, the corrections proposed by the translator in the "Addenda et Corrigenda" of the original edi-tions have for the most part been adopted. This text is in the public domain. You are free to do whatever you wish with it. Prepared for SuttaCentral by Bhikkhu Sujato.

SuttaCentral. (2020). Aṅguttara Nikāya 4.99. *Sikkhāpadasutta* Trainings. [Bhikkhu Thanissaro, Trans.]. Retrieved December 31, 2020, from https://suttacentral.net/an4.99/en/thanissaro. Translated from the Pāḷi by Thanissaro Bhikkhu. The text of this page is licensed under a Creative

Commons Attribution-NonCommercial 4.0 International License. To view a copy of the license, visit http://creativecommons.org/licenses/by-nc/4.0/. Documents linked from this page may be subject to other restrictions. Transcribed from a file provided by the translator. Access to Insight (Legacy Edition), 31 November 2013, http://www.accesstoinsight.org/. Prepared for SuttaCentral by Gabriel Laera and Ayya Vimala.

SuttaCentral. (2020). Aṅguttara Nikāya 8.62. *Alaṃsutta* Good Enough. [Bhikkhu Sujato, Trans.]. Retrieved December 31, 2020, from https://suttacentral.net/an8.62/en/sujato. Translated for SuttaCentral by Bhikkhu Sujato, 2018. Dedicated to the public domain via Creative Commons Zero (CC0). You are encouraged to copy, reproduce, adapt, alter, or otherwise make use of this translation in any way you wish. Attribution is appreciated but not legally required.

SuttaCentral. (2020). Saṃyutta Nikāya 47.4. *Sālasutta* At Sala. [Bhikkhu Bodhi, Trans.]. Retrieved December 31, 2020, from https://suttacentral.net/sn47.4/en/bodhi. The Connected Discourses of the Buddha (Wisdom Publications, 2000). This excerpt from The Connected Discourses of the Buddha by Bhikkhu Bodhi is licensed under a Creative Commons Attribution—Non Commercial—No Derivs 3.0 Unported License. Based on the work Connected Discourses of the Buddha at Wisdom Publications. Permissions beyond the scope of this license may be available at Wisdom Publications. Prepared for SuttaCentral by Blake Walsh.

SuttaCentral. (2020). Aṅguttara Nikāya 4.162. *Vitthārasutta* (Modes of Practice) in Detail. [Bhikkhu Thanissaro, Trans.]. Retrieved December 31, 2020, from https://suttacentral.net/an4.162/en/thanissaro. Translated from the Pāḷi by Thanissaro Bhikkhu. The text of this page is licensed under a Creative Commons Attribution-NonCommercial 4.0 International License. To view a copy of the license, visit http://creativecommons.org/licenses/by-nc/4.0/. Documents linked from this page may be subject to other restrictions. Transcribed from a file provided by the translator. Access to Insight (Legacy Edition), 31 November 2013, http://www.accesstoinsight.org/. Prepared for SuttaCentral by Gabriel Laera and Ayya Vimala.

SuttaCentral. (2020). Aṅguttara Nikāya 3.65. *Kesamuttisutta* Kesaputtiya. [Bhikkhu Bodhi, Trans.]. Retrieved December 31, 2020, from https://suttacentral.net/an3.65/en/bodhi. The Numerical Discourses of the Buddha (Wisdom Publications, 2012). This excerpt from The Numerical Discourses of the Buddha by Bhikkhu Bodhi is licensed under a Creative Commons Attribution-NonCommercial-NoDerivs 3.0 Unported License. Based on the work The Numerical Discourses of the Buddha at Wisdom Publications. Permissions beyond the scope of this license may be available at Wisdom Publications. Prepared for SuttaCentral by Blake Walsh.

SuttaCentral. (2020). Aṅguttara Nikāya 4.155. *Paṭisaṅkhānabalasutta* The Power of Reflection. [Bhikkhu Sujato, Trans.]. Retrieved December 31, 2020, from https://suttacentral.net/an4.155/en/sujato. Translated for SuttaCentral by Bhikkhu Sujato, 2018. Dedicated to the public domain via Creative Commons Zero (CC0). You are encouraged to copy, reproduce, adapt, alter, or otherwise make use of this translation in any way you wish. Attribution is appreciated but not legally required.

SuttaCentral. (2020). Itivuttaka 86. *Dhammānudhammapaṭipannasutta* Practice According to Dhamma. [J. D. Ireland, Trans.]. Retrieved December 31, 2020, from https://suttacentral.net/iti86/en/ireland. Translated from the Pāḷi by John D. Ireland. Digital Transcription Source: BPS Transcription Project. Extracted from The Udāna & the Itivuttaka, translated and introduced by John D. Ireland. Published in 1997. The complete book, including introduction and notes by the translator, is available from the Buddhist Publication Society. ISBN 955–24-0164-X. This text has been made available by the kind permission of the Buddhist Publication Socie-ty. It was released under the following licence terms: For free distribution. This work may be republished, reformatted, reprinted and redistributed in any medium. However, any such republication and redistribution is to be made available to the public on a free and unrestricted basis, and translations and other derivative works are to be clearly marked as such. Prepared for SuttaCentral by Bhikkhu Sujato.

SuttaCentral. (2020). Majjhima Nikāya 61. *Ambalaṭṭhikarāhulovādasutta* Advice to Rāhula at Ambalaṭṭhika. [Bhikkhu Sujato, Trans.]. Retrieved December 31, 2020, from https://suttacentral.net/mn61/en/sujato. Translated for SuttaCentral by Bhikkhu Sujato, 2018. Dedicated to the

Authored Texts

Bhikkhu Bodhi. (1999). *The noble eightfold path: The way to the end of suffering*. Buddhist Publication Society. https://www.accesstoinsight.org/lib/authors/bodhi/waytoend.html#pre.

Gombrich, R. F. (2013). *What the Buddha thought*. Equinox Publishing Ltd.

Hecker, H. (2009). *Similes of the Buddha*. Buddhist Publication Society. https://www.bps.lk/olib/bp/bp427s_Hecker_Similes-of-the-Buddha.pdf.

Killen, R. (2013). *Effective teaching strategies: Lessons from research and practice* (6th ed.). Cengage Learning Australia.

Krathwohl, D. R., Anderson, L. W., Mayer, R. E., Pintrich, P. R., Raths, J., & Wittrock, M. C. (2001). The taxonomy table. In L. W. Anderson, D. R. Krathwohl, P. W. Airasian, K. A. Cruikshank, R. E. Mayer, P. R. Pintrich, J. Raths, & M. C. Wittrock (Eds.), *A Taxonomy for learning, teaching, and assessing: A revision of Bloom's taxonomy of educational objectives* (pp. 27–37). Allyn & Bacon.

Ma Rhea, Z. (2012). Thinking Galtha, teaching literacy: From Aboriginal mother tongue to strangers' texts and beyond. In A. Cree (Ed.), *Aboriginal education: New pathways for teaching and learning* (pp. 24–53). Australian Combined University Press.

Nonaka, I. (1994). A dynamic theory of organizational knowledge creation. *Organization Science, 5*(1), 14–37. https://doi.org/10.1287/orsc.5.1.14.

Pichard, P., & Lagirarde, F. (Eds.). (2003). *The buddhist monastery: A cross-cultural survey*. École française d'Extrême-Orient.

Sujato, B., & Brahmali, B. (2015). *The authenticity of the early buddhist texts*. Chroniker Press. https://ocbs.org/wp-content/uploads/2015/09/authenticity.pdf.

SuttaCentral. (2020). *Acknowledgements*. Retrieved December 08, 2020, from SuttaCentral. https://suttacentral.net/acknowledgments.

Ven Nyanatiloka. (1988). *Buddhist dictionary: Manual of buddhist terms and doctrine* (4th ed., Reprinted). Buddhist Publication Society.

Appendix A
Glossary

I have collected together the key terms used by the Buddha to explain his educational philosophy, pedagogy, and core curriculum and given some further explanation than can be found in the main body of this text. The Glossary is not intended to be exhaustive. For key terminology, I have drawn on the treasure trove of definitions available at Sutta Central ([SC] 2020; https://suttacentral.net/) and the extensive Glossary that has been collated at *Access to Insight* ([AtI] https://www.accesstoinsight.org/glossary.html). I encourage the reader to also refer to additional reference texts as detailed.

Many reliable commentaries and discussions of the Buddha's teachings are to be found online in many languages and informed by many traditions. In keeping with the focus of this monograph, I have limited my discussion to the accepted meanings of key words within the Early Buddhist Texts. An excellent online resource that, in addition to its Glossary, provides deeper explanation of many of the ideas and terms used in this text can be found at Access to Insight ([AtI] 2020; https://www.accesstoinsight.org/ptf/index.html).

A

Ācariya	A teacher; an instructor (of religious texts); a teacher or a master; in some skill; an authority (https://suttacentral.net/define/ācariya).
Aññamañña paccaya	lit. 'in mutual conditionality' (BD, pp. 134–140), a central concept in the *Paṭiccasamuppādasutta* (SuttaCentral, 2020, SN 12.1), where the Buddha explains how suffering arises and how everything is *aññamañña paccaya* interdependent and mutually arising.
Aṭṭhaṅgikaṃ maggaṃ	lit. *aṭṭhaṅgika* having eight constituents, being made up of eight (intrinsic) parts and *-magga* path, meaning Eightfold

Z. M. Diamond, *Gautama Buddha*, https://doi.org/10.1007/978-981-16-1765-2

Path, conventionally called the Noble Eightfold Path (see Appendix A, this edition).

B

Brahma-vihāra — A divine state of mind; a name collectively given to the emotional states of *mettā* loving kindness, *karuṇā* compassion, *muditā* altruistic joy, and *upekkhā* equanimity, known as the Four Divine Abodes (Nyanatiloka, 1980, pp. 43–44).

C

Cattari ariya saccani — Four Noble Truths taught by the Buddha (see AtI, https://www.accesstoinsight.org/ptf/dhamma/sacca/index.html; see also, Appendix A, this edition).

D

Dhamma — A key term used extensively by the Buddha, as translated into Pāli meaning 'doctrine; nature; truth; the Norm; morality; good conduct' (https://suttacentral.net/define/dhamma); see also, *Dharma.*

Dhammabhāṇakas — Mentioned in the *Mahavamsa,* the ancient Sri Lankan Buddhist text, being those people who recited the *Dhamma* to help people remember the teachings. Carries the ancient Sanskrit meaning of one who is a public reader of sacred texts.

Dharma — Sanskrit spelling of the Pāli term *Dhamma;* used commonly as the translation into English versions of Mahayana teachings.

Dukkha — lit. suffering; pain; misery; agony; discomfort (SuttaCentral, 2020, https://suttacentral.net/define/dukkha; see also AtI 2020, https://www.accesstoinsight.org/ptf/dhamma/sacca/sacca1/dukkha.html).

F

Four Noble Truths — See *Cattari ariya saccani* (see also Appendix A, this edition).

K

Kalyāṇamitta A good friend; a person of fine qualities who is a friend, esp. in helping one to progress spiritually by his/her example and advice (SuttaCentral, 2020, https://suttacentral.net/define/kalyāṇamitta). I employ this term to denote the teacher as a reliable signpost, knowledgeable about the Buddha's teachings and having undertaken extensive practice, someone who knows the way because they have followed the same path.

M

Majjhimā paṭipadā *Majjhimā* carries the meaning of 'middle' (Buddhadatta Mahathera, 1958, p. 203). The word *paṭipadā* conveys a meaning of a 'line of conduct; mode of progress' (https://suttacentral.net/define/paṭipadā). In contemporary times, its English language translation of the 'Middle Way' is used to encapsulate the Buddha's key idea that nothing in education should be extreme, of either great discomfort, or great indulgence, but that the student should find the 'Middle Way' as the Buddha did. It is explained (SuttaCentral, 2020, para. 6) this way:

> *And what's the middle practice? It's when a mendicant meditates by observing an aspect of the body—keen, aware, and mindful, rid of desire and aversion for the world. They meditate observing an aspect of feelings ... They meditate observing an aspect of the mind ... They meditate observing an aspect of principles—keen, aware, and mindful, rid of desire and aversion for the world. This is called the middle practice.*

N

Nibbāna Lit. 'cooling; extinction (of a fire); emancipation; the final bliss' (https://suttacentral.net/define/nibbāna). The purpose of the Buddha's educational ideas was to enable people to cease from producing new karmic resultants that would cause the endless rounds of suffering to continue. To have achieved inner wisdom allowed a student to cool the fires to eventual extinction. In English, this concept is known as enlightenment.

Noble Eightfold Path — See *Aṭṭhaṅgikaṃ maggaṃ* (see also Appendix A, this edition).

P

Pacceka-buddha — A distinction is made within the Buddha's teaching between a person who achieves *nibbāna* during a life through their own efforts, a *pacceka-buddha* and, far rarer, one who having achieved *nibbāna* goes on to teach others becoming what is known as a Wheel-turning Buddha.

Pañca-sila — The Five Precepts, the core moral code of all Buddhists (see also AtI, 2005, https://www.accesstoinsight.org/ptf/dhamma/sila/pancasila.html).

Pañcavidyā — Five subjects studied at Nalanda University during the time of Xuanzang (602–664CE).

Pañña — wise; endowed with knowledge (https://suttacentral.net/define/pañña). In the Buddha's educational approach, the pursuit and development of inner wisdom was paramount. His pedagogy and curriculum were focussed on its cultivation and fruition.

Pariyatti — First stage of the *majjhimā patipadā* Middle Way approach developed by the Buddha, meaning accomplishment in the Scriptures, learning by heart of the holy texts (https://suttacentral.net/define/pariyatti). This stage emphasises learning from the teacher and from books.

Paṭiccasamuppāda — A core advanced teaching of the Buddha, meaning causal genesis; dependent origination (https://suttacentral.net/define/paṭiccasamuppāda). After a student had developed their understanding through following the Buddha's *majjhimā patipadā* Middle Way approach and the core curriculum of the *Buddha-Dhamma*, the student was introduced to more complex teachings that followed the same method.

Paṭipatti — Second stage of the *majjhimā patipadā* Middle Way approach developed by the Buddha, meaning 'conduct; practice; behaviour; religious practice' (https://suttacentral.net/define/paṭipatti). This stage emphasises practice and experience.

Paṭivedha — Third stage of the *majjhimā patipadā* Middle Way approach developed by the Buddha, meaning 'penetration; attainment; comprehension (https://suttacentral.net/define/paṭivedha). This stage emphasises the development of understanding based on experience through the development of discernment.

Pavīṇaupāya Lit. *pavīṇa* 'clever; skilful' (https://suttacentral.net/define/pavīṇa) and *-upāya* 'means, appropriate way' (https://suttacentral.net/define/upāya). This word combination is used here to denote in English translation the idea of pedagogy as 'skilful means' and also describes the teacher's overall approach to teaching the *Buddha-Dhamma.*

S

Sangha Lit. 'a multitude; an assemblage' (https://suttacentral.net/define/saṅgha). Over time, this word became used to denote the men and women who followed the Buddha's teachings, became *bhikkhus* monks and *bhikkhunis* nuns, and continued his work of education.

Sekha/Sekkha a learner; one who is in the course of perfection (https://suttacentral.net/define/sekha).

Sikkhā study; discipline (https://suttacentral.net/define/sikkhā).

Sikkhana learning; training (https://suttacentral.net/define/sikkhana).

Sikkhāpada code of training; instruction (https://suttacentral.net/define/sikkhāpada).

Sikkhāpaka/ Sikkhāpanaka a teacher; trainer (https://suttacentral.net/define/sikkhāpaka).

Sikkhāpana teaching; instruction (https://suttacentral.net/define/sikkhāpana).

Sutta This word has a wide range of meanings. In this text, I use it to denote a teaching given by the Buddha as a discourse or dialogue. It is also used to denote a chapter of the *Tipitaka* Buddhist Canon.

T

Tipitaka Meaning three baskets, translated into English as the Buddhist Canon. In this book, I concentrate my focus on the *Sutta Piṭaka* containing the core teachings of the Buddha and his explication of his educational philosophy and approach. The two other *Piṭaka* parts are the *Vinaya Piṭaka* containing the rules for the Saṅgha and the *Abhidhamma Pitaka*, the analytic exposition of the *Tipitaka* Buddhist Canon.

U

Ugganhāpeti teaches; instructs (https://suttacentral.net/define/ugganhāpeti).
Ugganhāti learns; takes up https://suttacentral.net/define/ugganhāti).
Ugganhiya having learnt or taken up (https://suttacentral.net/define/ugganhiya).

References

Suttas

SuttaCentral. (2020). Aṅguttara Nikāya 3.156–162. Retrieved 30 December 31, 2020, from https://suttacentral.net/an3.156-162/en/sujato. Translated for SuttaCentral by Bhikkhu Sujato, 2018. Dedicated to the public domain via Creative Commons Zero (CC0). You are encouraged to copy, reproduce, adapt, alter, or otherwise make use of this translation in any way you wish. Attribution is appreciated but not legally required.

Authored Texts

Buddhadatta Mahathera, A. P. (1958). Concise Pali-English dictionary (Reprinted) Singapore Buddhist Meditation Centre.

SuttaCentral. (2020). Early Buddhist texts, translations, and parallels. Retrieved December 31, 2020, from SuttaCentral. https://suttacentral.net/.

Ven Nyanatiloka. (1988). Buddhist dictionary: Manual of buddhist terms and doctrine (4th ed., Reprinted). Buddhist Publication Society.

Appendix B
Defining and Shaping the Buddha's Education Theories from Pāli and Sanskrit into English

While this monograph is predominantly written in Australian English, it draws on words and ideas that have been expressed by the Buddha in Sanskrit, Pal, and probably several other dialects and languages spoken in the region where he taught (for more detailed discussion, see Chap. 2 and Appendix A, Glossary, this edition).

The first question to consider is in what languages might the Buddha have taught. There has been considerable debate about this matter. Sujato and Brahmali (2015, p. 55) explain that:

> *In all probability, a similarly close relationship obtains between Pāḷi and the historical Buddha's own dialect. Moreover, the Buddha himself may have used varying dialects depending on where he travelled and certainly his disciples did: they were in fact encouraged to speak in their own dialect. As Buddhism spread throughout Northern India, this diverging use of language must eventually have led to a need for standardisation, and this probably explains the introduction and development of Pāḷi.*

Gombrich (2013) offers the following background information about the inter-relationship of these languages and dialects. Sanskrit is native to India. It is an Indo-European language and was first an oral language going back approximately to the year 2000 Before the Christian Era (BCE) and first written down in approximately 300 BCE. Its oldest texts are the Vedas that were preserved by the hereditary priestly caste known as the Brahmins. Prakrit is an Indian term for languages directly derived from Sanskrit. Pāḷi is a Prakrit language. Gombrich observes that Pāḷi was 'not exactly what the Buddha spoke but was fairly close to it' (Gombrich, 2013, p. xi) and it was the language used to orally first codify and then preserve in written texts over later years. Over time, the Pāḷi texts were preserved by what became known as the *Theravāda* Doctrine of the Elders Buddhist tradition. During the migration of Buddhist monks, nuns, and their ideas and practices across Asia (do be discussed in more detail in Chap. 3), the southern migration preserved the Buddha's teachings in the Pāḷi text as the authoritative source; a practice maintained into the contemporary era (Gombrich, 2013, p. xv). The development of these ideas after the Buddha's passing became known as *Mahayana* The Great Vehicle and the migration of these ideas across northern India and north and then east towards China and then Tibet

Z. M. Diamond, *Gautama Buddha*, https://doi.org/10.1007/978-981-16-1765-2

was preserved in Sanskrit, in addition to many northern Indian dialects together with the languages of the Indigenous peoples of the lands now known as Pakistan, Afghanistan, China, Korea, Japan, Indonesia, and Tibet. Initial orally-transmitted teachings memorised in both Sanskrit and Pāḷi were increasingly translated into local languages and dialects, work undertaken at Nalanda as it grew to university status and 'on the road' as Buddhist monks travelled the trade routes spreading the teachings and organising for them to be translated and eventually written down as the practice of writing developed. Echoing my previous point about how Buddhist has spread and found fertile soil in many geo-locations, Conze (1957, p. 77) observed that:

> *In Buddhism, there is nothing which cannot be easily transported from one part of the world to another. It can adapt itself as easily to the snowy heights of the Himalayas as to the parched plains of India, to the tropical climate of Java, to the moderate warmth of Japan ... Indians, Mongols and the blue-eyed Nordics of Central Asia could all adjust it to their own needs.*

In this monograph, I follow the practice of Sujato and Brahmali (2015) in using Pāḷi spelling of Indic terms, simply because I am more familiar with Pāḷi. In specific contexts, however, convenience or custom dictates my use of Sanskrit. Similarly, I adopt their approach to the use of the teachings of the Buddha by predominantly examining a body of work as described by them as being Early Buddhist Texts (EBTs), accepted in the main as being an authentic reflection, and possibly the actual words of the Buddha, and a reliable reflection of his ideas and intentions. In this, I follow Sujato and Brahmali (2015, pp. 9–10) who make the following definitional remarks:

> ***Early Buddhist Texts**: Texts spoken by the historical Buddha and his contemporary disciples. These are the bulk of the Suttas in the main four Pāḷi Nikāyas and parallel Āgama literature in Chinese, Tibetan, Sanskrit, and other Indian dialects; the pātimokkhas and some Vinaya material from the Khandhakas; a small portion of the Khuddaka Nikāya, consisting of significant parts of the Sutta Nipāta, Udāna, Itivuttaka, Dhammapada, and Thera- and Therīgāthā. The "Suttas". in a narrow sense are those passages that are directly attributed to the Buddha himself (and to a lesser extent his direct disciples).*
>
> ***Non-EBTs**: Abhidhamma, Mahāyāna Sūtras, Buddha biographies, historical chronicles, as well as the majority of the Khuddaka Nikāya and the Vinaya Piṭaka. The Jātakas are non-EBT but derive from stories that in some cases may even be earlier than the Buddha. Commentaries and other late texts may contain some genuine historical information alongside much later invention.*

I have also consulted numerous sources to provide a helpful understanding of the key Pāḷi and Sanskrit words that I have used in this book. For more detailed information, please refer to Appendix A, Glossary (this edition).

References

Conze, E. (1957). *Buddhism: Its essence and development*. Munshiram Manoharlal Publishers Pvt. Ltd.

Gombrich, R. F. (2013). *What the Buddha thought*. Equinox Publishing Ltd.

Sujato, Bhikkhu & Brahmali, Bhikkhu. (2015). *The authenticity of the early buddhist texts*. Chroniker Press. https://ocbs.org/wp-content/uploads/2015/09/authenticity.pdf.

Appendix C
Buddha-Dhamma Core Curriculum

The major scaffold for the Buddha's teachings is the *cattari ariya saccani* Four Noble Truths (*Dhammacakkappavattanasutta* SN 56.11, SuttaCentral, 2020; Story, 1961). The Buddha elaborated this framing of his ideas over many years, in a multitude of towns, villages, and temples and to thousands of people. As Venerable Thanissaro (1999, p. 1) explains,

> *The four noble truths are the most basic expression of the Buddha's teaching. As Ven. Śāriputra once said, they encompass the entire teaching, just as the footprint of an elephant can encompass the footprints of all other footed beings on earth.*

Books that preserve the corpus of the Buddha's teachings, the *Buddha-Dhamma* and commentaries about their meaning fill libraries and temples across the world into the present day. The Sangha of monks and nuns, together with laypeople, continue to teach aspects of this core curriculum according to their training and there is growing interest by teachers and parents in aspects such as awareness and mindfulness that are proving beneficial to children's development in the modern, formal education system. A deep examination of the *Buddha-Dhamma* core curriculum, while beyond the scope of this monograph, will provide the teacher with a reliable framework of content by which to develop a curriculum that would lay the groundwork for the development of wisdom in students, even in the modern classroom. The balancing of content knowledge, with an emphasis on personal experience and then a process of critical engagement with the experiences to foster deeper learning is important and as such, this text focuses on the pedagogical approach to teaching this *Buddha-Dhamma* core curriculum. The first three Truths lead to the most detailed exposition of eight steps in a pathway to the cultivation of wisdom.

The Budda introduces his idea about this very precise path, for example, in the *Maggaṅgasutta* (SN 43.11, SuttaCentral 2020, para. 1)

> *"... And what, bhikkhus, is the path leading to the unconditioned? The Noble Eightfold Path: this is called the path leading to the unconditioned."*

Z. M. Diamond, *Gautama Buddha*, https://doi.org/10.1007/978-981-16-1765-2

This path is known as the *aṭṭhaṅgikaṃ maggaṃ* Noble Eightfold Path (*Aṭṭhaṅgikasutta* SN 14.28, SuttaCentral, 2020, paras. 1–3). I quote it here in abbreviated versions of both Pāli and English:

> *Sāvatthiyaṃ viharati.*
>
> *"Dhātusova, bhikkhave, sattā saṃsandanti samenti. Micchādiṭṭhikā micchādiṭṭhikehi saddhiṃ saṃsandanti samenti; micchāsaṅkappā ... pe ... micchāvācā ... micchākammantā ... micchāājīvā ... micchāvāyāmā ... micchāsatino ... micchāsamādhino micchāsamādhīhi saddhiṃ saṃsandanti samenti.*
>
> *Sammādiṭṭhikā sammādiṭṭhikehi saddhiṃ saṃsandanti samenti; sammāsaṅkappā ... pe ... sammāvācā ... sammākammantā ... sammāājīvā ... sammāvāyāmā ... sammāsatino ... sammāsamādhino sammāsamādhīhi saddhiṃ saṃsandanti samentī"ti.*
>
> *At Sāvatthī.*
>
> *"Mendicants, sentient beings come together and converge because of an element: those of wrong view with those of wrong view ... wrong thought ... wrong speech ... wrong action ... wrong livelihood ... wrong effort ... wrong mindfulness ... wrong immersion ..."*
>
> *"Those who have right view ... right thought ... right speech ... right action ... right livelihood ... right effort ... right mindfulness ... right immersion with those who have right immersion."*

Bhikkhu Bodhi provides an extensive factorial analysis of the *aṭṭhaṅgikaṃ maggaṃ* Noble Eightfold Path that is a step-by-step guide to the pathway for the development of wisdom: (Bhikkhu Bodhi, 1984, pp. 131–136)

I. Samma ditthi—Right view

dukkhe nana—understanding suffering
dukkhasamudaye nana—understanding its origin
dukkhanirodhe nana—understanding its cessation
dukkhanirodhagaminipatipadaya nana—understanding the way leading to its cessation

II. Samma sankappa—Right intention

nekkhamma-sankappa—intention of renunciation
abyapada-sankappa—intention of good will
avihimsa-sankappa—intention of harmlessness

III. Samma vaca—Right speech

musavada veramani—abstaining from false speech
pisunaya vacaya veramani—abstaining from slanderous speech
pharusaya vacaya veramani—abstaining from harsh speech
samphappalapa veramani—abstaining from idle chatter

IV. Samma kammanta—Right action

panatipata veramani—abstaining from taking life
adinnadana veramani—abstaining from stealing
kamesu micchacara veramani—abstaining from sexual misconduct

V. Samma ajiva—Right livelihood

miccha ajivam pahaya—giving up wrong livelihood,
samma ajivena jivitam kappeti—one earns one's living by a right form of livelihood

VI. Samma vayama—Right effort

samvarappadhana—the effort to restrain defilements
pahanappadhana—the effort to abandon defilements
bhavanappadhana—the effort to develop wholesome states
anurakkhanappadhana—the effort to maintain wholesome states

VII. Samma sati—Right mindfulness

kayanupassana—mindful contemplation of the body
vedananupassana—mindful contemplation of feelings
cittanupassana—mindful contemplation of the mind
dhammanupassana—mindful contemplation of phenomena

VIII. Samma samadhi—Right concentration

pathamajjhana—the first jhana
dutiyajjhana—the second jhana
tatiyajjhana—the third jhana
catutthajjhana—the fourth jhana

References

Suttas

SuttaCentral. (2020). Saṃyutta Nikāya 43.11. *Maggaṅgasutta* The Eightfold Path. [Bhikkhu Bodhi, Trans.]. Retrieved December 31, 2020, from https://suttacentral.net/sn43.11/en/bodhi. The Connected Discourses of the Buddha (Wisdom Publica-tions, 2000). This excerpt from The Connected Discourses of the Buddha by Bhikkhu Bodhi is licensed under a Creative Commons Attribution—Non Commercial—No Derivs 3.0 Un-ported License. Based on the work Connected Discourses of the Buddha at Wisdom Publications. Permissions beyond the scope of this license may be available at Wisdom Publications. Prepared for SuttaCentral by Blake Walsh.

SuttaCentral. (2020). Saṃyutta Nikāya 14.28. *Aṭṭhaṅgikasutta* The Eightfold Path. [Bhikkhu Sujato, Trans.]. Retrieved December 31, 2020, from https://suttacentral.net/sn14.28/en/sujato. Translated for SuttaCentral by Bhikkhu Sujato, 2018. Dedicated to the public domain via Creative Commons Zero (CC0). You are encouraged to copy, reproduce, adapt, alter, or otherwise make use of this translation in any way you wish. Attribution is appreciated but not legally required.

SuttaCentral. (2020). Saṃyutta Nikāya 56.11. *Dhammacakkappavattanasutta* Setting in Motion the Wheel of the Dhamma. [Bhikkhu Bodhi, Trans.]. Retrieved December 31, 2020, from https://suttacentral.net/sn56.11/en/bodhi. The Connected Discourses of the Buddha (Wisdom Publications, 2000). This excerpt from The Connected Discourses of the Buddha by Bhikkhu Bodhi is licensed under a Creative Commons Attribution—Non Commercial—No Derivs 3.0 Un-ported License. Based on the work Connected Discourses of the Buddha at Wisdom Publications. Permissions beyond the scope of this license may be available at Wisdom Publications. Prepared for SuttaCentral by Blake Walsh.

Authored Texts

Bhikkhu Bodhi. (1984). *Noble eightfold path: The way to the end of suffering*. Buddhist Publication Society. Retrieved December 31, 2020, from https://www.bps.lk/olib/wh/wh308_Bodhi_Noble-Eightfold-Path.pdf.

Bhikkhu Thanissaro. (1999). *The four noble truths: A study guide*. Retrieved December 31, 2020, from https://www.accesstoinsight.org/lib/study/truths.html.

Story, F. (1961). *Foundations of Buddhism: The four noble truths*. Buddhist Publication Society. Retrieved December 31, 2020, from https://www.bps.lk/olib/wh/wh034_Story_Foundations-of-Buddhism--Four-Noble-Truths.pdf.